# The Essence of Alan Watts

# The Essence of Alan Watts

*Alan Watts*

*Celestial Arts*
*Millbrae, California*

*Cover and interior design by Betsy Bruno*

First printing July 1977

Made in the United States of America

photo of Alan Watts by Margo Moore
photo page 27 by Richard Borst

**Library of Congress Cataloging in Publication Data**

Watts, Alan Wilson, 1915-1973.
  The essence of Alan Watts.

    1. Philosophy — Collected works. I. Title.
B945.W321 1977    191    77-7724
ISBN 0-89087-210-4

1 2 3 4 5 6 7 8 — 82 81 80 79 78 77

# Contents

# THE STORY OF ALAN WATTS

For more than twenty years Alan Watts earned a reputation as the foremost interpreter of Eastern philosophies to the West. Beginning at the age of 20, when he wrote *The Spirit of Zen*, he developed an audience of millions who were enriched by his offerings through books, tape recordings, radio, television, and public lectures.

He wrote 25 books, each building toward a personal philosophy that he shared, in complete candor and joy, with his readers and listeners throughout the world. They presented a model of individuality and self-expression that can be matched by few contemporaries. His life and work reflect an astonishing adventure: he was editor, Anglican priest, graduate dean, broadcaster, and author-lecturer. He had fascinations for cooking, calligraphy, singing, and dancing. He held fellowships from Harvard University and the Bollingen Foundation and was Episcopal Chaplain at Northwestern University. He became professor and dean of the American Academy of Asian Studies in San Francisco, made the television series "Eastern Wisdom and Modern Life" for the National Educational Television, and served as visiting consultant to many psychiatric institutes and hospitals. He traveled widely with students in Japan.

Born in England in 1915, Alan Watts attended King's School Canterbury, served on the Council of the World Congress of Faiths (1936–38), and came to the United States in 1938. He held a Master's Degree in Theology from Seabury-Western Theological Seminary and an Honorary D.D. from the University of Vermont in recognition of his work in Comparative Religion.

Alan Watts died in 1973. *The Essence of Alan Watts*, a series of nine books in the unique *Celestial Arts* format, includes edited transcripts by his wife Mary Jane Watts of videotaped lectures that were produced by his friend, Henry Jacobs, and filmed by his son, Mark Watts, in the last years of his life.

# The Essence of Alan Watts

EGO

Photographs by Mike Powers and Maria Demarest

I suppose the most fascinating question in the world is: Who am I? Or, What am I? The seer, the knower, the one you are, is the most inaccessible of all experiences, completely mysterious and hidden.

We talk about *our* egos. We use the word *I*. I've always been tremendously interested in what people mean by the word *I* because it comes out in curious ways in speech. For instance, we don't say, "I am a body." We say, "I have a body." Somehow we don't seem to identify ourselves with all of ourselves. I say, "my feet," "my hands," "my teeth," as if they were something outside me. And as far as I can make out, most people feel that they are *something* about half way between the ears, and a little behind the eyes, inside the head, and from this center the rest of them sort of dangles. And the governing principle in there is what you call the ego. That's me!

But I just can't get rid of the idea that it's a hallucination. That's not what you are at all. And it's a very dangerous hallucination because it gives you the idea that you are a center of consciousness, energy, and responsibility that stands over against and in opposition to everything else. You are the principle inside your own body as if your body were an automobile and you the chauffeur. You feel caught in a trap because your body's something of a mess. It gets sick, tired, hurts, and eventually wears out and dies. You feel caught in the thing because you feel different from it.

3

Furthermore, you feel the world outside your body is an awful trap, full of stupid people, who are sometimes nice to you but mostly aren't. They're all out for themselves like you are and therefore there's one hell of a conflict going on. The rest of it, aside from people, is absolutely dumb—animals, plants, vegetables and rocks. Finally, behind the whole thing there are blazing centers of radioactivity called stars, and out there there's no air, there's no place for a person to live.

We have come to feel ourselves as centers of very, very tender, sensitive, vulnerable consciousness, confronted with a world that doesn't give a damn about us. And therefore, we have to pick a fight with this external world and beat it into submission to our wills. We talk about the conquest of nature; we conquer everything. We talk about the conquest of mountains, the conquest of space, the conquest of cancer, etc., etc. We're at war. And it's because we feel ourselves to be lonely ego principles, trapped in, somehow inextricably bound up with, a world that doesn't go our way unless somehow we can manage to force it to do so.

I feel this sensation of ourselves as an ego is a hallucination. A completely false conception of ourselves as an ego inside a bag of skin. What we really are is, first of all, the whole of our body. Although the body is bounded by a skin, I can differentiate between my outside and my inside. My body cannot exist except in a certain kind of natural environment. Obviously it requires air, and that air must be near a certain temperature, it requires nutrition; it requires that it be on a certain kind of planet near a certain kind of warm star spinning regularly around it in a harmonious and rhythmical way so that life can go on. That arrangement is just as essential to the existence of my body as to its own internal organs—my heart, my brain, my lungs, and so forth. So there really is no way of separating myself as a physical body from the natural environment in which I live.

4

Now, that means that I as a body go with my natural environment in the same way exactly as bees go with flowers. Bees look very different from flowers. The flower grows out of the ground, colors and perfumes the air. The bee is independent and buzzes around and flies. But where there are no bees, there are no flowers, and where there are no flowers, there are no bees. They go together and, in that sense, they make up a single system. Substitute for the word *system* the word *organism*, a single life form, a single individual, bees and flowers, however different they look. Naturally, my feet look very different from my head. Of course, a string is joining them and therefore we say, "well, it's all one, obviously." They are very different but they're both me. The feet and the head, though different, are like the bees and the flowers—they go with each other.

Therefore, to define myself in a scientific way, to make a clear description of my body, my organism, my behavior, and describe what it's doing, must also describe the environment, the surroundings in which it is doing it. In other words, it would be meaningless to describe myself as walking if I didn't describe the ground. Because if I didn't describe the ground, my description of walking would simply be of a person swinging his legs in empty space. That wouldn't be walking—I have to describe the ground on which I walk.

What I am is a transaction or an interaction between this organism and its surrounding environment. They go together and constitute what we call in physics, a unified field. And that's what I am from a purely physical, scientific point of view. It may involve many more things than that, but I am an organism/environment.

7

But that's not what my ego feels like. That's not the average commonsensical conception of *I*. Because *I* is associated with the organism and not with the environment. It is opposing the environment, and it is not associated with all of the organisms. As I said, the ego tends to regard the rest of the organism as the chauffeur does the automobile.

How do we get this false sensation of being an ego? Well, it seems to me that it's made up of two things and the first thing we have to understand is that in the course of civilization we confuse our ideas and words and symbols about the world with the world itself. The General Semantics group, founded by Dr. Alfred Korzybski, have a little song. . "Oh, the word is not the thing, the word is not the thing, hi, ho, the derry-o, the word is not the thing." Obviously you can't get wet from the word *water*. The image, the idea, the symbol, the word is not the reality, The ego, what we feel as *I*, consists of the image or idea of ourselves we see in a mirror, or by listening to ourselves played back on a tape recorder or television.

When I was a little boy I remember I had a friend up the street called Peter, and I admired him very much. Sometimes I came home and imitated Peter's behavior. My mother would say to me, "Alan, that's not you, that's Peter." You see, she was giving me an image of myself. When I did anything terrible she would say, "Alan, it's just not like you to do that." She was busy building in me an image, an idea of the kind of act I was supposed to put on, the kind of person I was supposed to be.

8

The word *person* comes from the Latin *persona*, which means that through which (*per*) the sound (*sona*) goes. It referred originally to the masks worn by actors in classical drama, because those masks had megaphonic mouths, so that in the open-air theater they would project the sound. So the *persona*, the person, is the mask, is the role you're playing. And all your friends and relations and parents and teachers are busy telling you who you are, what your role in life is, and there are only a certain number of acceptable roles you can play.

First of all then, your sense of *I* is your sense of who you are, whether you're tinker, tailor, soldier, sailor, rich man, poor man, beggarman, thief, whether you're a clown, strong and silent, a clinging vine—we can name dozens of them—you identify yourself with a certain way of acting. It's quite complicated, but nevertheless there's a certain way of acting with which you identify yourself and which constitutes your image.

The image of yourself that you have is a social institution in the same way as it is, for example, a social institution to divide the day into twenty-four hours, or to divide the foot into twelve inches, or to draw lines of latitude and longitude which are purely imaginary over the surface of the earth. It's very useful to do that because these lines are the means of navigation, but there are no lines of latitude and longitude on or over the earth—they are imaginary. You cannot, for example, use the equator to tie up a package, because it's an abstract, imaginary line. And in just the same way, your image of yourself as an ego is an imaginary concept that is not the organism and furthermore, is not this organism in its inseparable relationship to its whole physical and natural environment.

The image of yourself that you have is simply a caricature! A caricature is an excellent example: When we make a caricature of Adolf Hitler, we pull down the hair and put a comb under his nose instead of a mustache. In the same way, our image of ourselves is a caricature of ourselves because it does not include almost all the important things about ourselves; it does not include all the goings-on inside the physical organism. Oh, we get belly-rumbles; occasionally we're aware of our breathing; occasionally we're aware that it hurts somewhere. But for the most part we're totally unconscious of everything going on inside us. We're unconscious of our brains and how they work. We're unconscious of our relationships to the external world, many of our relationships to other people are completely unconscious. We depend on telephone operators, electricians supplying our electricity, on all kinds of service that we never even think about. We don't think about air pressure. We don't think about the chemical composition of the air we breathe, we don't think about cosmic rays, gamma rays, X-rays, the output of the sun. All these things are absolutely essential to our life but they are not included in the ego image.

So the ego image is very incomplete. In fact, it's an illusion. But we say, "Now, look, it can't be that way, because I feel *I*, I mean, it's not just an image of myself I have; I have a solid feeling behind the word *I*, when I think *I*, I feel there's something there." What is that? Interesting question. Because if your brain is your ego, you have very little in the way of direct sensation of your brain. In fact, operations can be performed on the brain with only surface anesthesia—there's no feeling in the brain itself. Therefore, the brain cannot be the sensation of ego.

When your eyes are functioning well you don't see your eyes. If your eyes are imperfect you see spots in front of them. That means there are some lesions in the retina or wherever, and because your eyes aren't working properly, you feel them. In the same way, you don't hear your ears. If you have a ringing in your ears it means there's something wrong with your ears. Therefore, if you do feel yourself, there must be something wrong with you. Whatever you have, the sensation of *I* is like spots in front of your eyes—it means something's wrong with your functioning. That's why you feel you're there, why you feel you as being different from, somehow cut off from, all that you really are, which is everything you're experiencing. The real you is the totality of everything you're aware of and a great deal more besides.

But what is this thing that we feel in ourselves when we say, "That is the concrete, material me"? Well, I'll tell you what it is. When you were a little child in school, you were picking your nose and looking out the window or flicking spit balls or something, suddenly the teacher rapped the desk, "Pay attention!" Now, how did you pay attention? Well, you stared at the teacher, and you wrinkled your brow, because that's how you look when you pay attention. And when the teacher sees all the pupils in the class staring and frowning, then the teacher is consoled and feels the class is paying attention. But the class is doing nothing of the kind. The class is pretending to pay attention.

15

You're reading a book; there's some difficult book you have to read because it's required. You're bored to death with it, and you think, "Well, I've really got to concentrate on this book." You glare at it, you try to force your mind to follow it's argument, and then you discover you're not really reading the book—you're thinking about how you ought to read it. What do you do if I say to you, "Look, take a hard look at me, take a real hard look." Now what are you doing? What's the difference between a hard look and a soft look? Why, with your hard look, you are straining the muscles around your eyes, and you're starting to stare. If you stare at a distant image far away from you, you'll make it fuzzy. If you want to see it clearly you must close your eyes, imagine black for awhile, and then lazily and easily open them and you'll see the image. The light will come to you. And what do you do if I say, "Now, listen carefully, listen very carefully to what I'm saying." You'll find you're beginning to strain yourself around the ears.

I remember in school there was a boy who couldn't read. He sat next to me in school, and he wanted to convince the teacher that he really was trying to read. He would say, "rrruuunnn, ssspppooottt, rrruuunnn." He was using all his muscles. What have they got to do with reading? What does straining your muscles to hear have to do with hearing? Straining your muscles to see, what's that got to do with seeing? Nothing.

Supposing somebody says, "O.K. now, you've got to use your will, you've got to exercise strong will." That's the ego, isn't it. What do you do when you exercise your will? You grit your teeth, you clench your fists. If you want to stop wayward emotions you go uptight. You pull your stomach in, or hold your breath, or contract your rectal muscles. But all these activities have absolutely nothing to do with the efficient functioning of your nervous system. Just as staring at images makes them fuzzy, listening hard with all this muscular tension distracts you from what you're actually hearing; gritting your teeth has nothing to do with courage, all this is a total distraction. And yet we do it all the time; we have a chronic sensation of muscular strain, the object of which is an attempt to make our nervous system, our brains, our sensitivity function properly—and it doesn't work.

It's like taking off in a jet plane. You're going zooming down the runway and you think, "This plane has gone too far down the runway and it isn't up in the air yet," so you start pulling at your seatbelt to help the thing up. It doesn't have any effect on the plane. And so, in exactly the same way, all these muscular strains we do and have been taught to do all our lives long, to look as if we're paying attention, to look as if we're trying, all this is futile. But the chronic sensation of strain is the sensation to which we are referring as *I*.

So our ego is what? An illusion married to a futility. It's the image of ourselves, which is incorrect, false, and only a caricature, married to, combined with, a futile muscular effort to will our effectiveness.

19

Wouldn't it be much better if we had a sensation of ourselves that was in accord with the facts? The facts, the reality of our existence, is that we are both the natural environment, which ultimately is the whole universe, and the organism playing together. Why don't we feel that way? Why, obviously because this other feeling gets in the way of it. This socially induced feeling which comes about as a result of a kind of hypnotism exercised upon us throughout the whole educational process has given us a hallucinatory feeling of who we are, and therefore we act like madmen. We don't respect our environment; we destroy it. But you know, exploiting and destroying your environment, polluting the water and the air and everything, is just like destroying your own body. The environment is your body. But we act in this crazy way because we've got a crazy conception of who we are. We're raving mad.

"Well," you ask, "how do I get rid of it?" And my answer to that is, that's the wrong question. How does what get rid of it? You can't get rid of your hallucination of being an ego by an activity of the ego. Sorry, but it can't be done. You can't lift yourself up by your own bootstraps. You can't put out fire with fire. And if you try to get rid of your ego with your ego, you'll just get into a vicious circle. You'll be like somebody who worries because they worry, and then worries because they worry because they worry, and you'll go round and round and get crazier than ever.

The first thing to understand when you say, "What can I do about getting rid of this false ego?" is that the answer is "nothing," because you're asking the wrong question. You're asking, "How can I, thinking of myself as an ego, get rid of thinking of myself as an ego?" Well, obviously you can't. Now, you say, "Well then, it's hopeless." It isn't hopeless. You haven't got the message, that's all.

20

If you find out that your ego feeling, your will and all that jazz, cannot get rid of that hallucination, you've found out something very important. In finding out that you can't do anything about it, you have found out that you don't exist. That is to say, you as an ego, you don't exist so obviously you can't do anything about it. So you find you can't really control your thoughts, your feelings, your emotions, all the processes going on inside you and outside you that are happenings—there's nothing you can do about it.

So then, what follows? Well, there's only one thing that follows: You watch what's going on. You see, feel, this whole thing happening and then suddenly you find, to your amazement, that you can perfectly well get up, walk over to the table, pick up a glass of milk and drink it. There's nothing standing in your way of doing that. You can still act, you can still move, you can still go on in a rational way, but you've suddenly discovered that you're not what you thought you were. You're not this ego, pushing and shoving things inside a bag of skin.

You feel yourself now in a new way as the whole world, which includes your body and everything that you experience, going along. It's intelligent. Trust it.

Imagine the world coming suddenly out of nothing. Close your eyes and listen and you will hear silence and then sounds coming out of that silence. Now use your eyes and see light, shape, form coming at you as a vibration that is proceeding out of space.

Our logic resists such concepts because common sense tells us we can't get something out of nothing. Normally we think of all the energetic manifestations of this universe as coming out of the past; the things that *were* here are producing the things that *are* here now. But I want you to look at it the other way so that you can see the whole world starting now instead of in the past, and the past as a kind of echo fading away into memory, like the wake of a ship that trails across the water and then fades out. But the wake is started by the ship in the present. In the same way, I am moving on to the uncommonsensical idea of the world as a production of energy that is beginning right now and is coming out of the nothing that we variously call space and silence.

How on earth could that happen? The usual explanation is that the world is being created by God. In Christian theology it is said that God creates the world out of nothing. I want to emphasize the point, in all fairness to Catholic, Islamic, and Jewish doctrine, that it doesn't merely teach that God once upon a time started the world and set it going like you would wind up a machine and then leave it alone. These religions teach that God is always creating the world out of nothing and willing it by his divine energy into being at this moment.

Now the difficulty for most of us—especially for educated people—in the modern world is that the old-fashioned idea of God has become incredible or implausible. In church or in synagogue, we seem to be addressing a royal personage. The layout looks like a royal court. There is some sort of throne, and we address prayers and requests to the being represented by the alter, throne, or tabernacle as if that being were a king and were causing this universe in his royal, omnipotent, and omniscient wisdom.

But then, when we take a look through our telescopes and microscopes or when we just look at nature, we have a problem. Because the idea of God that we get from the holy scriptures, the Bible, the Koran, doesn't quite seem to fit the world around us in just the same way you wouldn't ascribe a composition by Stravinsky to Bach. The style of God venerated in church, mosque, and synagogue seems completely different from the style of the natural universe. It's so hard to conceive the author of the one as the author of the other.

Furthermore, it strikes most intelligent people that our traditional religious ideas of God are primitive. It seems naive to think that this universe could have been authored by a sort of old gentleman who lives far above the stars in heaven, seated on a golden throne and adored by legions of angels. That is a concept unworthy of the sort of universe modern science has revealed to us.

I have a picture of God. A friend of mine photographed a statue of him in a church just south of Oaxaca in Mexico. It shows a primitive Indian-Catholic image of God the Father wearing a triple crown like the Pope, only he's rather young and handsome. He's not like the old, gray-bearded man. This is a serious Christian idol of God the Father Almighty. This is what has become implausible.

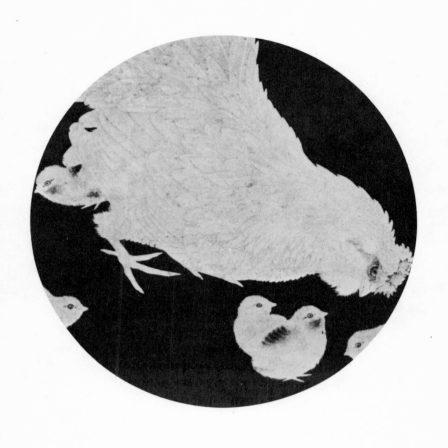

But also for many people it has become implausible that the root of the universe, which the theologian Paul Tillich calls the *ground of being*, can be in some way a person to whom we can relate in the same way that we relate to other people—a person who cares about us.

Jesus said, "Five sparrows are sold for a farthing. But yet not one of them falls to the ground without the Father knowing it. So realize that you are of more value than many sparrows." In other words, God cares a great deal more about you. But it just baffles our imagination that there could be this sort of person, who cares about each one of us, who is totally aware of every single thing that we are and that we do and, by virtue of being aware of us, creates us.

Of course, one thing that is difficult about the idea is that it's embarrassing. We do not feel comfortable if we are watched all the time by an infinitely intelligent judge. Imagine you are a child in school and you're working at some exercise and the teacher walks behind your desk and looks at what you're doing. Even if you like the teacher very much, you feel put down by being watched; it makes you self-conscious and awkward. Many people opt for atheism for the same reason, because they don't want the uncomfortable feeling that they're being watched all the time. It's awkward. And if I were God I wouldn't do it. I wouldn't want to embarrass my creatures in that way, so I would leave them alone for a lot of the time.

The kind of god that people worship is, of course, an attempt to imagine an absolutely perfect human being. But it's a very poor attempt. For example, Jesus taught that if somebody sins against you, forgive him. His disciples asked, "How many times do you forgive him?" And Jesus answered, "Ninety and nine times," *always* forgive somebody who sins against you. But notice, that what is required of a saint—a saint is always forgiving—is not required of God. God will not forgive you unless you apologize, and you have to grovel on the ground if you've committed what the Catholic church calls a mortal sin. You have to come to God in a state of great penitence and if you don't you are liable to be confined in the dungeons of the court of Heaven, commonly known as Hell, for always and always and always.

Now, I don't think that's a very nice kind of fellow. You wouldn't invite that sort of God to dinner. He would embarrass everybody! When God would look at you, you would feel you were being seen through and through, and that all your awful past, all your falseness, would be completely perceptible to him. And though he understood it and forgave it he would nonetheless make you feel absolutely terrible. You just wouldn't want that sort of company at dinner.

You may think it's frivolous of me to describe such a situation, but don't forget the pictorial image of God that people have in the backs of their minds. Even if you're a very sophisticated philosopher or theologian, that primitive pictorial image has a very strong influence on your feelings about religion, about the universe, and about yourself. This is the reason that the traditional idea of God has become implausible to many people.

Modern Protestant theologians, and even some Catholics, have been talking recently about the death of God and about the possibility of a religionless religion, a religion which does not involve belief in God. What would become of the Gospel of Jesus Christ if it were shown that Jesus' own belief in God was unnecessary and invalid? What would remain of his teachings? Of his ideas about caring for other human beings, about social responsibility and so on. I think that would be a pretty wishy-washy kind of religion. If you're going to say that this life is fundamentally nothing but a pilgrimage from the maternity ward to the crematorium and that's it, baby, you've had it, I think that indicates a singular lack of imagination. I would like to look at the death-of-God theology in an entirely different way. What is dead is not God but an idea of God, a particular conception of God that has died in the sense of becoming implausible. And I find this a very good thing.

The Greek word in the New Testament for a sin is *antinomic* or *anomia* and that means to miss the point or, as in archery, to miss the mark. And therefore, from the Mosaic Ten Commandments comes the idea that it is a sin, a missing of the point, to substitute an idol for God.

Then, the statue of God I described is an idol. But even those Mexican-Indians, don't seriously confuse that particular image with God. The danger of it is they may think of God in the form of man. But the images that have been made of God out of wood and stone and in painting have never really been taken seriously as actually what God is like. Nobody has confused the actual image of Buddha for the statues commonly seen in the East. Buddha is never identified with a god because Buddha is a human being, and these images are never seriously confused with what they represent any more than a Catholic confuses a crucifix with Jesus Christ.

The images of God that are tangible are not really very dangerous. The dangerous images of God are those that we make, not out of wood and stone, but out of ideas and concepts. Sir Thomas Aquinas, for example, defined God as a necessary being, He who is necessarily. That is a philosophical concept; but that concept is an idol because it confuses God with an idea. Because an idea is abstract it seems much more spiritual than an image made of wood or stone. That's precisely where it becomes deceptive.

Many people think that the Bible is the authentic word of God and they worship the Bible, making it into an idol. They disregard the ironical remark of Jesus to his contemporary Jews, "You search the scriptures daily, for in them you think you have life." And as St. Paul said later, "The letter kills, but the spirit gives life." So whatever you put as an image or an idea in the place of God necessarily falsifies God.

A lot of people say, "I don't think I could face life unless I could believe in a just and loving god." It strikes me that that kind of belief in God is actually expressing a lack of faith. The word belief in Anglo-Saxon comes from the Anglo-Saxon root *lief* which means to wish. So belief really means a strong wish. When you say the creed, "I believe in God, the Father Almighty, maker of heaven and earth and of all things seen and unseen," you are really saying: *"I fervently wish that there exists* God the Father Almighty, creator of heaven and earth, etc." Because, if you really have faith you don't need belief, because faith is an entirely different attitude from belief.

Faith is a state of openness or trust. To have faith is like when you *trust* yourself to the water. You don't grab hold of the water when you swim, if you go stiff and tight in the water you sink. You have to relax. Thusly, the attitude of faith is the very opposite of clinging, of holding on. In other words, a person who is a fanatic in religion, one who simply has to believe in certain propositions about the nature of God and of the universe is a person who has no faith at all—he's holding on tight.

Although Martin Luther made such a thing about faith, he wrote a hymn —in German, *Ein fest Burg ist unser Gott*, "A Mighty Fortress is our God." That's not a hymn of faith! A person of faith doesn't need a fortress; he's not on the defensive.

In the same way, many churches are designed like the royal courts of kings. In the church design called the basilica, which means the court of a basileus or king, the bishop sits at the back in his throne and all his attendant clergy stand around him like his guards in a court. Why is this? A king stands with his back to the wall because he rules by force. And when his subjects and his courtiers approach him they prostrate themselves, they kneel down. Why? Because that's a difficult position from which to start a fight. Are we projecting the image of a frightened king as being the godhead?

The usual Protestant church, on the other hand, looks like a courthouse. The minister wears a black gown as is worn by a judge, and there are pews and pulpits and all the familiar wooden boxes of court furniture. And the minister, like the judge, throws the book at you! He preaches the law laid down in that other idol of God, the Bible. But does God need all that? Is God somebody who takes this aggressive attitude either of the king in court where all the subjects must prostrate, or of the judge who bangs the gavel and interprets the law? This is ridiculous! And a God so conceived is an idol and manifests the absence of faith of all those who worship him because they demonstrate no attitude of trust. They cling to these rules, to these conceptions, and have no fundamental adaptability to life.

You might say that a good scientist has more faith than a religious person, because a good scientist says, "My mind is open to the truth, whatever the truth may turn out to be. I have no preconceptions, but I do have some hypotheses in my mind as to what the truth might be, and I'm going to test them." And the test is to open all the senses to reality and find out what that reality is. But then again, the scientist runs into a problem because he knows that whatever comes to him as reality depends on the structure of his instruments and his senses, and ultimately the structure of his brain. So he has to have faith in his own brain, faith in himself, faith that his physical organism including his mind is indeed reliable and will determine reality, truth—what is.

You have to believe your reason, your logic, your intelligence. You have to have faith in them even though you can't ultimately check on yourself to make certain you're operating properly. It's not like your mind is a radio and can be fixed by screwing in a new connection here and there— you always have to trust.

Therefore, one could say that the highest image of God is the unseen behind the eyes—the blank space, the unknown, the intangible and the invisible. That is God! We have no image of that. We do not know what that is, but we have to trust it. There's no alternative. You can't help trusting it. You've got to.

That trust in a God whom one cannot conceive in any way is a far higher form of faith than fervent clinging to a God of whom you have a definite conception. That conception can easily be wrong and, even if it's right, clinging to it would be the wrong attitude, because when you love someone very much you shouldn't cling to them.

In a New Testament story Mary Magdalene, who loved Jesus very much, is said to have seen him after his resurrection, and she immediately ran to cling to him. And he said, "Do not touch me," but the Greek word *hatir* means to cling to. Don't *cling* to me! Don't cling to anything of the spirit. Don't cling to the water, because the more you grab it the faster it will slip through your fingers. Don't cling to your breath, you'll get purple in the face and suffocate. You have to let your breath out. That's the act of faith, to breathe out, and it will come back. The Buddhist word *nirvana* actually means to breathe out; letting go is the fundamental attitude of faith.

It isn't as if Christians haven't been aware of this. One of the most fundamental sourcebooks of Christian spirituality, *Theologia Mystica*, was written in the sixth century by an Assyrian monk, Dionysius Exiguus. It is a very strange document, because it explains that the highest knowledge of God is through what he calls in Greek *agnostos*, which means unknowing. One knows God most profoundly, the most truly, in not knowing God.

MEDITATION

Photographs by Joseph McHugh

The art of meditation is a way of getting into touch with reality. And the reason for meditation is that most civilized people are out of touch with reality. They confuse the world as it is with the world as they think about it, talk about it, and describe it. For on the one hand there is the real world and on the other a whole system of symbols about that world which we have in our minds. These are very, very useful symbols; all civilization depends on them. But like all good things, they have their disadvantages, and the principle disadvantage of symbols is that we confuse them with reality in the same way as we confuse money with actual wealth, and our names, ideas, and images of ourselves with ourselves.

Of course, reality from a philosopher's point of view is a dangerous word. A philosopher will ask what do I mean by *reality*—am I talking about the physical world of nature, or am I talking about a spiritual world, or what? I have a very simple answer: When we talk about the material world, that is actually a philosophical concept. In the same way, if I say that reality is spiritual, that's also a philosophical concept. And reality itself is not a concept. Reality is......(Sound of a gong). And we won't give it a name.

It's amazing what doesn't exist in the real world. For example, in the real world there aren't any things, nor are there any events. That doesn't mean the real world is a perfectly featureless blank! It means that it is a marvelous system of wiggles in which we descry things and events in the same way as we would project images on a Rorschach blot or pick out particular groups of stars in the sky and call them constellations. Well, there are groups of stars in our mind's eye in our system of concept, but they are not out there as constellations already grouped in the sky. In the same way, the difference between myself and all the rest of the universe is nothing more than an an idea—it is not a real difference. Meditation is a way in which we come to feel our basic inseparability from the whole universe. What that requires is that we shut up. We become interiorly silent and cease from the interminable chatter that goes on inside our skulls.

Most of us think compulsively all the time; we talk to ourselves. If I talk all the time I don't hear what anyone else has to say. In exactly the same way, if I think all the time, that is to say if I talk to myself all the time, I don't have anything to think about except thoughts. Therefore, I'm living entirely in the world of symbols and I'm never in relationship with reality. I want to get in touch with reality: That's the basic reason for meditation.

There is another reason, and this is a bit more difficult to understand. We could say that meditation doesn't have a reason or doesn't have a purpose. In this respect it's unlike almost all other things that we do except perhaps making music and dancing. When we make music we don't do it in order to reach a certain point, such as the end of the composition. If that were the purpose of music then obviously the fastest players would be the best. Also, when we are dancing we are not aiming to arrive at a particular place on the floor as in taking a journey. When we dance, the journey itself is the point, as when we play music the playing itself is the point. And exactly the same thing is true in meditation. Meditation is the discovery that the point of life is always arrived at in the immediate moment.

Therefore, if you meditate for an ulterior motive, that is to say to improve your mind, to improve your character, to be more efficient in life, you've got your eye on the future and you are not meditating. The future is a concept—it doesn't exist! There is no such thing as tomorrow! There never will be because time is always now. That's one of the things we discover when we stop talking to ourselves and stop thinking. We find there is only a present, only an eternal now.

One meditates for no reason at all except for the enjoyment of it. Here I would interpose the essential principle that meditation is supposed to be fun—it's not something you do as a grim duty. The trouble with religion today is that it is so mixed up with grim duties. You do it because it is *good for you*. It's a kind of self-punishment. Meditation when correctly done has nothing to do with all that. It's a kind of *digging* the present. It's a kind of *grooving* with the eternal now, it brings us into a state of peace where we can understand that the point of life, the place where it's at, is simply here and now.

The art of meditation uses various props or supports which should be mentioned. The first thing we are going to use as a means of stilling chatter in the mind is pure sound. And for that reason it is useful to have a gong. I have a Japanese Buddhist gong made of bronze and shaped like a bowl. You may buy one or make your own. Or you can use your own voice, chanting.

The second prop is a string of beads. These beads are used in meditation for an unconscious method of timing yourself. Instead of looking at a watch you move a bead each time you breathe in and out. And when you get to a certain rate of slow breathing, counting half the 108 beads on a rosary takes about 40 minutes. That is the usual length of time one sits in meditation, otherwise you become uncomfortable and get stiff legs and problems of that kind.

A third prop in meditation is the use of incense. The sense of smell is our repressed sense. Because it's our repressed sense, it has a very powerful influence on us and I will discuss it at length at the end of this book. Unconsciously we associate certain smells with certain states of mind, and since the smell of incense is associated with peace and contemplation, it's advantageous to burn incense in meditation.

Another thing that we should discuss is how does one sit in meditation. You can sit any way you want—you can sit in a chair, or you can sit like I sit which is the Japanese way, kneeling with the toes pointing behind and sitting on the heels in an upright posture, hands lying loosely in the lap. Or you can sit in the lotus position, which is more difficult, cross-legged with the feet on the thighs, soles upwards—and the younger you begin practicing this the easier you find it to do. You can just sit cross-legged on a raised cushion above the floor if you prefer. The point is if you keep your back erect—I don't mean stiff nor slumped—you are centered and easily balanced and have the feeling of being rooted to the ground. That sort of physical stability is very important for the avoidance of distraction and generally feeling settled, here and now. "Je suis, je reste," as the French say, "I'm here and I'm going to stay."

Now that you are sitting and have your props, the easiest way to get into the meditative state is to begin listening. Simply close your eyes and allow yourself to hear all the sounds that are going on around you, listen to the general hum and buzz of the world as if you were listening to music. Don't try to identify the sounds you are hearing, don't put names on them, simply allow them to play with your ear-drums. Let them go. In other words, let your ears hear whatever they want to hear. Don't judge the sounds—there are no proper sounds nor improper sounds, and it doesn't matter if somebody coughs or sneezes or drops something—it's all just sound.

As you pursue that experiment you will very naturally find that you can't help naming sounds, identifying them, and go on thinking, talking to yourself inside your head, automatically. But it's important that you don't try to repress those thoughts by forcing them out of your mind because that will have precisely the same effect as if you were trying to smooth rough water with a flatiron—you're just going to disturb it all the more. What you do is this: As you hear sounds coming into your head, thoughts, you simply listen to them as part of the general noise going on just as you would be listening to cars going by, or to birds chattering outside the window. So look at your own thoughts as just noises. And soon you will find that the outside world and the inside world come together. They are a happening. Your thoughts are a happening just like the sounds going on outside, and everything is simply a happening and all you are doing is watching it.

In this process another happening that is very important is that you're breathing. As you start meditation you allow your breath to run just as it wills. In other words, don't do any breathing exercise, just watch your breath breathing the way it wants to breathe. And then notice a curious thing: You say in the ordinary way *I breathe* because you feel that breathing is something you are doing voluntarily just as you might be walking or talking. But you will also notice that when you are not thinking about breathing, your breathing goes on just the same. So the curious thing about breath is that it can be looked at both as a voluntary and an involuntary action. You can feel, on the one hand, *I am doing it* and, on the other hand, *it is happening to me*. And so, breathing is a most important part of meditation because it is going to show you, as you become aware of your breath, that the hard and fast division we make between what we do and what happens to us is arbitrary.

Watch your breathing and become aware that both the voluntary and the involuntary aspects of your experience are all one happening. That may at first seem a little scary. You may think *am I just the puppet of a happening, the mere passive witness of something that's going on completely beyond my control?* or *am I really doing everything that's going along?* If I were, I should be God and that would be very embarrassing because I would be in charge of everything—that would be a terribly responsible position! The truth of the matter is both things are true. Everything is happening to you, and you are doing everything. For example, your eyes are turning the sun into light, it's the nerve ends in your skin turning electric vibrations in the air to heat and temperature, it's your eardrums that are turning vibrations in the air into sound. This is the way in which you are creating the world. But when we're not talking about it, when we're not philosophizing about it, then there is just this happening, this...(Sound of a gong)...and we won't give it a name.

When you breathe for a while, just letting it happen and not forcing it in any way, you will discover a curious thing: Without making any effort you can breathe more and more deeply. Breathing out is important because it's the breath of relaxation as when we say, "Whew!" and heave a sigh of relief. So when you are breathing out you get the sensation that your breath is falling out. Dropping, dropping, dropping out with the same sort of feeling you would have if you were settling down into an extremely comfortable bed, you just get as heavy as possible and let yourself go. You let your breath go out in just that way. And when it's thoroughly, comfortably out and feels like coming back again, you don't pull it back in, you let it fall back in, letting your lungs expand, expand, expand until they feel very comfortably full. You wait a moment and let it stay there and then once again you let it fall out. In this way you will discover that your breath becomes naturally easier and easier and slower and slower, and more and more powerful.

Now you are listening to sound, listening to your own interior feelings and thoughts, and watching your breath all just as happenings that are neither voluntary nor involuntary. You are simply aware of these basic sensations. Then you begin to be in the state of meditation. Don't hurry anything, don't worry about the future, don't worry about what progress you're making. Be entirely content to be aware of what is. Don't be selective—"I should think of this and not that." Just watch whatever is happening.

To make this somewhat easier, to have the mind free from discursive, verbal thinking, chanted sound is extremely useful. If you, for example, simply listen to a gong, let that sound be the whole of your experience. It's quite simple, it requires no effort. And then along with that, or alone if you don't have a gong, you can use what in the Sanskrit language is called mantra. Mantras are chanted sounds which are used not for their meaning but for the simple tone, and they go along with slow breathing. One of the basic mantras is, of course, the word spelled OM. That sound is used because it runs from the back of your throat to your lips and contains the whole range of the voice and—it represents the total energy of the universe. This word is called the *pranava*, the name for the Ultimate Reality, for which than which there is no whicher. And so in this way then, if you chant it, *Ahhhhhhuuummmmmm.* And vary it *Ahhhhhhmmmmm*, *Ahummmmmmmm*, and keep it up for quite a long time and find that the words will become pure sound. You won't be thinking about it, you won't have any images about the sound going on in your mind. You will become completely absorbed in the sound and find yourself living in an eternal now in which there is no past and there is no future, and there is not difference between what you are as knower and what you are as the known, between yourself and the world of nature outside you. It all becomes one doing, one happening.

In addition to those slow moving chants you may find, according to your temperament, it is easier to do a fast moving one. These have a rhythm that is absorbing. A chant that you may have heard goes *Hari Krishna, Hari Krishna, Krishna Krishna, Hari Hari, Hari Krishna, Hari Krishna, Krishna Krishna, Hari Hari, Hari Rama Hari Rama, Rama Rama, Hari Hari, Hari Krishna, Hari Krishna, Krishna Krishna, Hari Hari...* And it doesn't matter what it means (Actually Krishna and Rama are the names of Hindu divinities.) The point is to get with that thing that is running, running, running... *Hari Krishna, Hari Krishna, Krishna Krishna, Hari Hari* and so on.

If you're a Christian or a Jew you may feel more inclined to use a meditation word that is more congenial to you, *Halleluja, Halleluja, Halleluja...*

If you are a Mohammedan you can use the Allah, the name of God. They have a way of doing it which gets very exciting: *Al-lah, Al-lah, Al-lah, Al-lah, Al-lah, Al-lah, Al-lah, Al-lah, Al-lah, Al-lah, Al-lah, Al-lah, Al-lah, Al-lah, Al-lah, Al-lah, Al-lah, Al-lah, Al-lah, Al-lah, Al-lah, Al-lah, Al-lah, Al-lah, Al-lah, Al-lah, Al-lah, Al-lah, Al-lah, Al-lah, Al-lah, Al-lah, Al-lah, Al-lah Al-lah Al-lah Al-lah Al-lah Al-lah Al-lah Al-lah Al-lah...* And it gets faster and faster and after 40 minutes you will be out of your mind.

But you see, to go out of your mind at least once a day is tremendously important. By going out of your mind you come to your senses. And if you stay in your mind all the time, you are overrational. In other words, you are like a very rigid bridge which because it has no give, no craziness in it, is going to be blown down in the first hurricane.

# INCENSE

Trying to convey the idea of smells to you in words has the same sort of frustration one gets trying to describe color to the blind. I have a friend who was born blind. She has no idea what darkness is. And so I had to try to give her an idea of what stars are and why we love them. I said, "Imagine when you touch the edge of something, you feel the edge, and then you move your hand away and nothing obstructs your hand, so there is space, nothing obstructing. Now imagine if you could put your hands out and feel around yourself a large collection of randomly distributed prickles, sharp points, that don't hurt you. At least not like the point of a needle. They're kind of pleasure-pain. We get this impression with the things we call our eyes, a friendly prickle coming at us from all over space when we can see them at night." So we try and translate the language of sight into the language of touch. Likewise we have this difficulty in talking about smell to people who, as G. K. Chesterton said, "They haven't got no noses, and goodness only knowses the noselessness of man."

Our sense of smell is not only repressed but is the one that we aren't really very proud of. For example, if I ask you "Do you smell?" It seems to be a rude question. There's a famous story about that great English literatus, Dr. Johnson, who got into a stagecoach one day (this was in the eighteenth century when people didn't bathe as much as they do today) and, shortly after, a lady got onto the stagecoach and sat opposite him, and said to him, "Sir, you smell." He said, "On the contrary, madam, you smell. I stink." And so you see how even in those times the word smell had a bad odor. There are only four adjectives in the English language that apply specifically to the sense of smell. We have acrid, pungent, fragrant, and putrid. We have ever so many adjectives from taste which we apply to smell, as when we say something smells sweet, or something of that kind. But we really aren't very conscious of the sense of smell. And yet it exercises an enormous influence upon us just because we're not conscious of it. I believe that instant likes and dislikes that we have for other people that are sometimes completely irrational are based on an unconscious determination of whether we do or don't like their smell. Smells are so powerful in evoking memories! Things you smelled as a child, say the smell of fresh coffee being cooked early in the morning, bacon frying, leaves being burned on an autumn day, all evoke vivid emotions and feelings of childhood.

But when people talk about very deep things, they never talk about the sense of smell. They talk about touch, vision, taste, and hearing. For example, we hear about the vision of God. In the Catholic Church it is said that the highest thing to which man can attain or to which the angels can attain is the beatific vision, to see God. One of the Psalms says, "Oh taste and see how excellent the Lord is." Taste and see. But no one ever had the idea of smelling God, of having not just the beatific vision, but the beatific aroma. Yet curiously enough, throughout the whole history of religions, until we got to what is called the phenomenon of the Protestant nose, we've used incense in our religious services.

Hindus use incense, Buddhists use incense, Mohammedans use incense, Catholics use incense, Hebrews use incense or used to. But there came a break at the time of the Reformation when incense was somehow given up. And why is this? Why this repression of the sense of smell? I don't know, but I do know that it is repressed. That's a shame! We're depriving ourselves of a whole world of wonder. The nose is just as sensitive as the ears, and the same way as there can be glories for the eyes, there can be glories for the nose. I don't know why we're so diffident, so uptight about admitting that we have noses. Animals have the most incredible sense of smell and can detect all sorts of things. They open up to themselves a whole new world of experience by simply using their noses. Now if you don't use your nose, you're really in just as pitiable a condition as somebody who was born blind or deaf. You've lost a whole sense. So there is a whole art of smell. I know very little about one half of it: The art of perfumery. But I do know that a very skilled manufacturer of perfumes gets a very beautiful lady, sniffs the odor of her body and combines the natural odor of her body with a perfume ingredient that will be its perfect partner, producing some entirely individual scent that is her own authentic smell. I don't know why you shouldn't have your own authentic smell just as you have your own authentic voice, your own authentic face, and, indeed, your own authentic character. However, I do know quite a bit about incense.

Everybody knows that incense is widely sold in the United States and Europe. But the ordinary incense sold is usually black or purple in color. And although there are good incenses that are black and purple, I advise you never to buy a black or a purple incense, unless you're buying from someone who really understands incense and can advise you what to buy. But ordinarily, black or purple incenses smell like cheap perfume. A bad incense always has a soapy smell; a good incense has a woodsy, resinous, or floral smell. The absolutely basic incense for the Orient is sandalwood. I have a small trunk of sandalwood on which are written the Chinese characters, "Bird, Sound; Flower, Perfume." So, from the bird—sound, from the flower—perfume. Sometimes a piece of sandalwood is made into a statue, such as a Hindu goddess. But generally speaking, sandalwood is the basic incense. It comes in various forms—chips, powder, and sticks. The best way to burn incense is in a bowl with sand. Use charcoal, which you can buy from ecclesiastical shops, impregnated with saltpeter that lights itself. You can use ordinary barbecue charcoal but I don't recommend it. When you get the charcoal going, take a chip of incense wood and place it on the charcoal and slowly it will heat up. Soon you'll find the whole room marvelously impregnated with this curiously sweet, woodsy smell that isn't icky-sweet.

There are three basic kinds of incense: temple incense, punk for scaring off insects, and boudoir incense. Temple incense is very pure; it has the feeling of high mountain forests, or loneliness—the chip form of sandalwood. There's the powder form of sandalwood which you just pinch on the lighted charcoal. You can use powdered sandalwood for rubbing into your hands. I wear round my neck what the Japanese call a juzu. It's a Zen Buddhist rosary. And you rub a little sandalwood powder into your hands and you play with it. I use them for counting my breath during meditation. You just breathe in and out on each bead, once out and once in. After you've counted each bead your whole rosary is perfumed with sandalwood.

Another wonderful kind of wooden incense comes from a tree, which the Japanese call gingko, found in the Orient that gets a disease which causes the wood to become extremely hard. And that very hard wood, aloeswood is enormously expensive. The disease in the tree is like the pearls in the oyster—somehow out of disease comes something beautiful. And you can burn aloeswood on charcoal. It has one of the most marvelous perfumes in the world. Its smell is the high forest, and old Dr. Suzuki, the great authority on Zen Buddhism, said, "The smell of gingko is the smell of Buddhism." It is used in Buddhist temples in China and Japan for special occasions. There are so many other fantastic varieties. There is a special incense which the Japanese use in the peculiar custom of tea ceremony. It's a ceremony that is nonreligious and yet very religious. Tea ceremony is drinking tea, and there are no images, icons, or religious symbols present. There is just drinking of tea in a completely, fully attentive way, as if it were the only important thing in the universe. Tea ceremony is completely living in the present, being absolutely with what you're doing, but in a kind of relaxed, easy way. Living in the eternal now, which is actually the only place there is to be. For the ceremony the Japanese use a particular vase with a curious little ivory top. Originally it was a jar for pills or herbal medicine. The masters of the tea ceremony felt that they were so elegant that they came to be used as incense containers for the ceremony. The incense is made of very small, black balls with an absolutely distinctive smell that is associated with the tea ceremony.

Another familiar form of incense is stick incense. Stick incense is lighted, the flame blown out, and stuck in a bowl of sand. The most luxurious of Japanese incense is based on musk although it's green, which is usually pine. Also, you can find, although it's rare, amazing stick incense from Tibet. It's regarded as a punk. Punk has the smell of autumn leaves. It is a little richer and is very good for keeping away mosquitoes. There is a similar, marvelous incense stick from Nepal. It is a coarse incense that I have a special liking for, it is distinct from the ones that are too icky-perfumed. One of the most extraordinary ones from Nepal comes in the form of a little piece of rope. This has a good-sweet flavor as distinct from icky-sweet. It's like the sweetness of fresh strawberries or fine honey compared to the sweetness of cheap candy.

Pakistan has a spiral incense which is a punk, used for keeping away mosquitoes. There's another interesting form of spiral incense which is used to reproduce a religious symbol, or whatever, when lighted it burns until the symbol is outlined in black.

In the West, the principal incense in use is resin. Frankincense, a resin, is really basic to incenses used in the Christian churches both of the East and of the West. And the delightful thing about using frankincense is the censer or thurible which you swing to disperse the incense. It's charming to use, and you can swing it right around without the incense coming out. It is used this way throughout the Western churches and, for reasons unknown to me, the Protestants gave it up. They lost all the joy of doing this thing for the greater glory of God.

NOTHINGNESS

Photographs by Joseph McHugh

$M$y home is aboard the ferryboat Vallejo which is tied up at the north end of Sausalito close to San Francisco. You may think a ferryboat is a rather weird place to live. But I've always loved weird things. When I was a little boy, people used to say to me, "Alan, you're so weird. Why can't you be like other people?" I thought that was just plain dull, like having the same thing for dinner every day. And, it is well said, variety is the spice of life.

Some things are weird because they are obvious—nobody ever thinks of them. Some of the most fascinating scientific discoveries have been made by people who questioned what was accepted as common sense. Like "Anybody can see that the earth is flat and people know it's flat." The questioning of that fundamental assumption was the beginning of geography.

73

When I consider the weirdest of all things I can think of, do you know what it is? *Nothing.* The whole idea of nothing is something that has bugged people for centuries, especially in the Western world. We have a saying in Latin, *Ex nihilo nihil fit,* which means, "Out of nothing comes nothing." In other words, you can't get something out of nothing. It's occurred to me that this is a fallacy of tremendous proportions. It lies at the root of all our common sense, not only in the West, but in many parts of the East as well. It manifests as a kind of terror of nothing, a putdown on nothing, a putdown on everything associated with nothing such as sleep, passivity, rest, and even the feminine principle which is often equated with the negative principle (although women's lib people don't like that kind of thing, when they understand what I'm saying I don't think they'll object). To me, nothing—the negative, the empty—is exceedingly powerful. I would say, not *Ex nihilo nihil fit,* but, "You can't have something without nothing."

How do we basically begin to think about the difference between something and nothing? When I say there is a cigar in my right hand and there is no cigar in my left hand, we get the idea of *is,* something, and *isn't,* nothing. At the basis of this reasoning lies the far more obvious contrast of solid and space. We tend to think of space as nothing; when we talk about the conquest of space there's a little element of hostility. But actually, we're talking about the conquest of distance. Space or whatever it is that lies between the earth and the moon, and the earth and the sun, is considered to be just nothing at all.

74

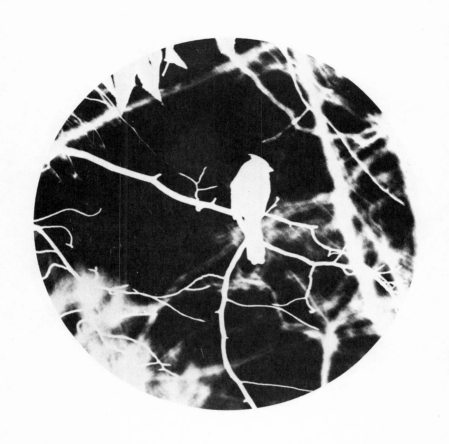

But to suggest how very powerful and important this nothing at all is, let me point out that if you didn't have space, you couldn't have anything solid. Without space outside the solid you wouldn't know where the solid's edges were. For example, you can see me in a photograph because you see a background and that background shows up my outline. But if it weren't there, then I and everything around me would merge into a single, rather peculiar mass. You always have to have a background of space to see a figure. The figure and the background, the solid and the space, are inseparable and go together.

We find this very commonly in the phenomenon of magnetism. A magnet has a north pole and a south pole— there is no such thing as a magnet with one pole only. Supposing we equate north with *is* and south with *isn't*. You can chop the magnet into two pieces, if it's a bar magnet, and just get another north pole and south pole, another *is* and *isn't*, on the end of each piece.

What I am trying to get into basic logic is that there isn't a sort of fight between something and nothing. Everyone is familiar with the famous words of Hamlet, "To be or not to be, that is the question." It isn't; to be or not to be is not the question. Because you can't have a solid without space. You can't have an *is* without an *isn't*, a something without a nothing, a figure without a background. And we can turn that round, and say, "You can't have space without solid."

Imagine nothing but space, space, space, space with nothing in it, forever. But there you are imagining it and you're something in it. The whole idea of there being only space, and nothing else at all, is not only inconceivable but perfectly meaningless, because we always know what we mean by contrast.

We know what we mean by white in comparison with black. We know life in comparison with death. We know pleasure in comparison with pain, up in comparison with down. But all these things must come into being together. You don't have first something and then nothing or first nothing and then something. Something and nothing are two sides of the same coin. If you file away the tails side of a coin completely, the heads side of it will disappear as well. So in this sense, the positive and negative, the something and the nothing, are inseparable—they go together. The nothing is the force whereby the something can be manifested.

We think that matter is basic to the physical world. And matter has various shapes. We think of tables as made of wood as we think of pots as made of clay. But is a tree made of wood in the same way a table is? No, a tree *is* wood; it isn't *made* of wood. Wood and tree are two different names for the same thing.

But there is in the back of our mind, the notion, as a root of common sense, that everything in the world is made of some kind of basic *stuff*. Physicists, through centuries, have wanted to know what that was. Indeed, physics began as a quest to discover the basic stuff out of which the world is made. And with all our advances in physics we've never found it. What we have found is not stuff but form. We have found shapes. We have found structures. When you turn up the microscope and look at things expecting to see some sort of stuff, you find instead form, pattern, structure. You find the shape of crystals, beyond the shapes of crystals you find molecules, beyond molecules you find atoms, beyond atoms you find electrons and positrons between which there are vast spaces. We can't decide whether these electrons are waves or particles and so we call them wavicles.

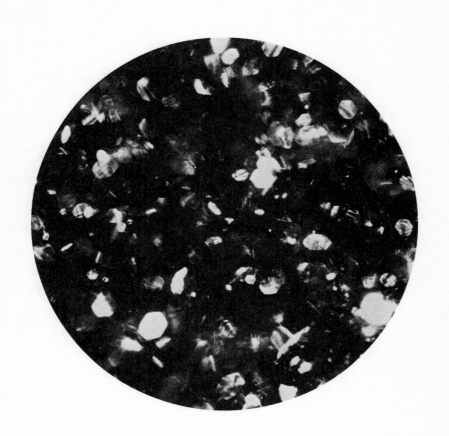

What we will come up with will never be stuff, it will always be a pattern. This pattern can be described, measured, but we never get to any stuff for the simple reason there isn't any. Actually, stuff is when you see something unclearly or out of focus, fuzzy. When we look at it with the naked eye it looks just like goo. We can't make out any significant shape to it. But when you put it under the microscope, you suddenly see shapes. It comes into clear focus as shape.

And you can go on and on, looking into the nature of the world and you will never find anything except form. Think of stuff; basic substance. You wouldn't know how to talk about it; even if you found it, how would you describe what it was like? You couldn't say anything about a structure in it, you couldn't say anything about a pattern or a process in it, because it would be absolute, primordial goo.

What else is there besides form in the world? Obviously, between the significant shapes of any form there is space. And space and form go together as the fundamental things we're dealing with in this universe. The whole of Buddhism is based on a saying, "That which is void is precisely form, and that which is form is precisely void." Let me illustrate this to you in an extremely simple way. When you use the word *clarity*, what do you mean? It might mean a perfectly polished lens, or mirror, or a clear day when there's no smog and the air is perfectly transparent like space.

What's the next thing *clarity* makes you think of? You think of form in clear focus, all the details articulate and perfect. So the one word *clarity* suggests to you these two apparently completely different things: the clarity of the lens or the mirror, and the clarity of articulate form. In this sense, we can take the saying "Form is void, void is form" and instead of saying *is*, say *implies*, or the word that I invented *goeswith*. Form always goeswith void. And there really isn't, in this whole universe, any substance.

Form, indeed, is inseparable from the idea of energy, and form, especially when it's moving in a very circumscribed area, appears to us as solid. For example, when you spin an electric fan the empty spaces between the blades sort of disappear into a blur, and you can't push a pencil, much less your finger, through the fan. So in the same way, you can't push your finger through the floor because the floor's going too fast. Basically, what you have down there is nothing and form in motion.

I knew of a physicist at the University of Chicago who was rather crazy like some scientists, and the idea of the insolidity, the instability of the physcial world, impressed him so much that he used to go around in enormous padded slippers for fear he should fall through the floor. So this commonsense notion that the world is made of some kind of substance is a nonsense idea—it isn't there at all but is, instead, form and emptiness.

Most forms of energy are vibration, pulsation. The energy of light or the energy of sound are always on and off. In the case of very fast light, very strong light, even with alternating current you don't notice the discontinuity because your retina retains the impression of the *on* pulse and you can't notice the *off* pulse except in very slow light like an arc lamp. It's exactly the same thing with sound. A high note seems more continuous because the vibrations are faster than a low note. In the low note you hear a kind of graininess because of the slower alternations of on and off.

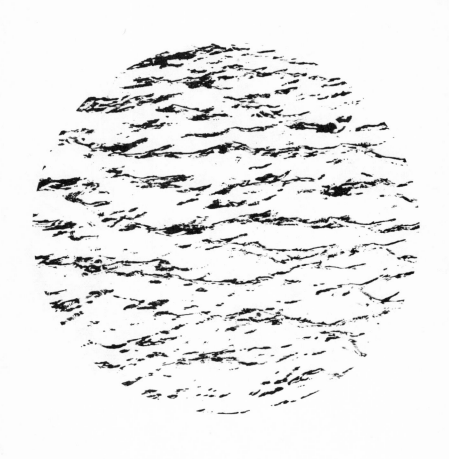

All wave motion is this process, and when we think of waves, we think about crests. The crests stand out from the underlying, uniform bed of water. These crests are perceived as the things, the forms, the waves. But you cannot have the emphasis called a crest, the concave, without the de-emphasis, or convex, called the trough. So to have anything standing out, there must be something standing down or standing back. We must realize that if you had this part alone, the up part, that would not excite your senses because there would be no contrast.

The same thing is true of all life together. We shouldn't really contrast existence with nonexistence, because actually, existence is the alternation of now-you-see-it/now-you-don't, now-you-see-it/now-you-don't, now-you-see-it/now-you-don't. It is that contrast that presents the sensation of there being anything at all.

Now, in light and sound the waves are extraordinarily rapid so that we don't hear or see the interval between them. But there are other circumstances in which the waves are extraordinarily slow, as in the alternation of day and night, light and darkness, and the much vaster alternations of life and death. But these alternations are just as necessary to the being of the universe as in the very fast motions of light and sound, and in the sense of solid contact when it's going so rapidly that we notice only continuity or the *is* side. We ignore the intervention of the *isn't* side, but it's there just the same, just as there are vast spaces within the very heart of the atom.

Another thing that goes along with all this is that it's perfectly obvious that the universe is a system which is aware of itself. In other words, we, as living organisms, are forms of the energy of the universe just as much as the stars and the galaxies, and, through our sense organs, this system of energy becomes aware of itself.

But to understand this we must again relate back to our basic contrast between on and off, something and nothing, which is that the aspect of the universe which is aware of itself, which does the awaring, does not see itself. In other words, you can't look at your eyes with your eyes. You can't observe yourself in the act of observing. You can't touch the tip of a finger with the tip of the same finger no matter how hard you try. Therefore, there is on the reverse side of all observation a blank spot; for example, behind your eyes from the point of view of your eyes. However you look around there is blankness behind them. That's unknown. That's the part of the universe which does not see itself because it is seeing.

We always get this division of experience into one-half known, one-half unknown. We would like to know, if we could, this always unknown. If we examine the brain and the structure of the nerves behind the eyes, we're always looking at somebody else's brain. We're never able to look at our own brain at the same time we're investigating somebody else's brain.

So there is always this blank side of experience. What I'm suggesting is that the blank side of experience has the same relationship to the conscious side as the *off* principle of vibration has to the *on* principle. There's a fundamental division. The Chinese call them the *yang*, the positive side, and the *yin*, the negative side. This corresponds to the idea of one and zero. All numbers can be made of one and zero as in the binary system of numbers which is used for computers.

86

And so it's all made up of off and on, and conscious and unconscious. But the unconscious is the part of experience which is doing consciousness, just as the trough manifests the wave, the space manifests the solid, the background manifests the figure. And so all that side of life which you call unconscious, unknown, impenetrable, *is* unconscious, unknown, impenetrable because it's really you. In other words, the deepest you is the nothing side, is the side which you don't know.

So, don't be afraid of nothing. I could say, "There's nothing in nothing to be afraid of." But people in our culture are terrified of nothing. They're terrified of death; they are uneasy about sleep, because they think it's a waste of time. They have a lurking fear in the back of their minds that the universe is eventually going to run down and end in nothing, and it will all be forgotten, buried and dead. But this is a completely unreasonable fear, because it is just precisely this nothing which is always the source of something.

Think once again of the image of clarity, crystal clear. *Nothing* is what brings *something* into focus. This *nothing*, symbolized by the crystal, is your own eyeball, your own consciousness.

DEATH

Photographs by Mike Powers and Maria Demarest

I've always been fascinated with the idea of death as far back as I can remember, from earliest childhood. You may think that's kind of morbid, but when a child at night says the phrase *If I should die before I wake,* there's something about it that's absolutely weird. What would it be like to go to sleep and never wake up? Most reasonable people just dismiss the thought. They say, "You can't image that"; they shrug their shoulders and say, "Well, that will be that."

But I'm one of those ornery people who aren't content with an answer like that. Not that I'm trying to find something else beyond that, but I am absolutely fascinated with what it would be like to go to sleep and never wake up. Many people think it would be like going into the dark forever or being buried alive. Obviously it wouldn't be like that at all! Because we know darkness by contrast, and only by contrast, with light.

I have a friend, a girl, who is very intelligent and articulate, who was born blind and hasn't the faintest idea what darkness is. The word means as little to her as the word light. So it is the same for you; you are not aware of darkness when you are asleep.

If you went to sleep, into unconsciousness for always and always, it wouldn't be at all like going into the dark; it wouldn't be at all like being buried alive. As a matter of fact, it would be as if you had never existed at all! Not only you, but everything else as well. You would be in that state, as if you had never been. And, of course, there would be no problems, there would be no one to regret the loss of anything. You couldn't even call it a tragedy because there would be no one to experience it as a tragedy. It would be a simple—nothing at all. Forever and for never. Because, not only would you have no future, you would also have no past and no present.

At this point you are probably thinking, "Let's talk about something else." But I'm not content with that, because this makes me think of two other things. First of all, the state of nothingness makes me think that the only thing in my experience close to nothingness is the way my head looks to my eye. I seem to feel there is a world out there confronting my eye, and then behind my eye there isn't a black spot, there isn't even a hazy spot. There's nothing at all! I'm not aware of my head, as it were, as a black hole in the middle of all this luminous visual experience. It doesn't even have very clear edges. The field of vision is an oval, and behind this oval of vision there is nothing at all. Of course, if I use my fingers and touch I can feel something behind my eyes; if I use the sense of sight alone there is just nothing there at all. Nevertheless, out of that blankness, I see.

92

The second thing it makes me think of is when I'm dead I am as if I never had been born, and that's the way I was before I was born. Just as I try to go back behind my eyes and find what is there I come to a blank, if I try to remember back and back and back to my earliest memories and behind that—nothing, total blank. But just as I know there's something behind my eyes by using my fingers on my head, so I know through other sources of information that before I was born there was something going on. There were my father and my mother, and their fathers and mothers, and the whole material environment of the Earth and its life out of which they came, and behind that the solar system, and behind that the galaxy, and behind that all the galaxies, and behind that another blank—space. I reason that if I go back when I'm dead to the state where I was before I was born, couldn't I happen again?

What has happened once can very well happen again. If it happened once it's extraordinary, and it's not really very much more extraordinary if it happened all over again. I do know I've seen people die and I've seen people born after them. So after I die not only somebody but myriads of other beings will be born. We all know that; there's no doubt about it. What worries us is that when we're dead there could be nothing at all forever, as if that were something to worry about. Before you were born there was this same nothing at all forever, and yet you happened. If you happened once you can happen again.

Now what does that mean? To look at it in its very simplest way and to properly explain myself, I must invent a new verb. This is the verb *to I*. We'll spell it with the letter *I* but instead of having it as a pronoun we will call it a verb. The universe *I's*. It has *I'd* in me it *I's* in you. Now let's respell the word *eye*. When I talk about *to eye*, it means to look at something, to be aware of something. So we will change the spelling, and will say the universe *I's*. It becomes aware of itself in each one of us, and it keeps the *I'ing*, and everytime it *I's* every one of us in whom it *I's* feels that he is the center of the whole thing. I know that you feel that you are I in just the same way that I feel that I am I. We all have the same background of nothing, we don't remember having done it before, and yet it has been done before again and again and again, not only before in time but all around us everywhere else in space is everybody, is the universe *I'ing*.

Let me try to make this clearer by saying it is the universe *I'ing*. Who is *I'ing*? What do you mean by *I*? There are two things. First, you can mean your ego, your personality. But that's not your real *I'ing*, because your personality is your idea of your self, your image of yourself, and that's made up of how you feel yourself, how you think about yourself thrown in with what all your friends and relations have told you about yourself. So your image of yourself obviously isn't you any more than your photograph is you or any more than the image of *anything* is *it*. All our images of ourselves are nothing more than caricatures. They contain no information for most of us on how we grow our brains, how we work our nerves, how we circulate our blood, how we secrete with our glands, and how we shape our bones. That isn't contained in the sensation of the image we call the ego, so obviously, then the ego image is not my self.

My self contains all these things that the body is doing, the circulation of the blood, the breathing, the electrical activity of the nerves, all this is me but I don't know how it's constructed. And yet, I do all that. It is true to say I breathe, I walk, I think, I am conscious—I don't know how I manage to be, but I do it in the same way as I grow my hair. I must therefore locate the center of me, my *I'ing*, at a deeper level than my ego which is my image or idea of myself. But how deep do we go?

We can say the body is the *I*, but the body comes out of the rest of the universe, comes out of all this energy—so it's the universe that's *I'ing*. The universe *I's* in the same way that a tree apples or that a star shines, and the center of the appling is the tree and the center of the shining is the star, and so the basic center of self of the *I'ing* is the eternal universe or eternal thing that has existed for ten thousand million years and will probably go on for at least that much more. We are not concerned about how long it goes on, but repeatedly it *I's*, so that it seems absolutely reasonable to assume that when I die and this physical body evaporates and the whole memory system with it, then the awareness that I had before will begin all over once again, not in exactly the same way, but that of a baby being born.

Of course, there will be myriads of babies born, not only baby human beings but baby frogs, baby rabbits, baby fruit flies, baby viruses, baby bacteria—and which one of them am I going to be? Only one of them and yet every one of them, this experience comes always in the singular one at a time, but certainly one of them. Actually it doesn't make much difference, because if I were born again as a fruit fly I would think that being a fruit fly was the normal ordinary course of events, and naturally I would think that I was an important person, a highly cultured being, because fruit flies obviously have a high culture. We don't even know how to look at it. But probably they have all sorts of symphonies and music, and artistic performances in the way light is reflected on their wings in different ways, the way they dance in the air, and they say, "Oh, look at her, she has real style, look how the sunlight comes off her wings." They in their world think they are as important and civilized as we do in our world. So, if I were to wake up as a fruit fly I wouldn't feel any different than I do when I wake up as a human being. I would be used to it.

Well, you say, "It wouldn't be me! Because if it were me again I would have to remember how I was before!" Right, but you don't know, remember, how you were before and yet you are content enough to be the me that you are. In fact, it's a thoroughly good arrangement in this world that we don't remember what it was like before. Why? Because variety is the spice of life, and if we remembered, remembered, remembered having done this again and again and again we should get bored. In order to see a figure you have to have a background, in order that a memory be valuable you also have to have a *forgettory*. That's why we sleep every night to refresh ourselves; we go into the unconscious so that coming back to the conscious is again a great experience.

Day after day we remember the days that have gone on before, even though there is the interval of sleep. Finally there comes a time when, if we consider what is to our true liking, we will want to forget everything that went before. Then we can have the extraordinary experience of seeing the world once again through the eyes of a baby—whatever kind of baby. Then it will be completely new and we will have all the startling wonder that a child has, all the vividness of perception which we wouldn't have if we remembered everything forever.

The universe is a system which forgets itself and then again remembers anew so there's always constant change and constant variety in the span of time. It also does it in the span of space by looking at itself through every different living organism, giving an all-around view.

That is a way of getting rid of prejudice, getting rid of a one-sided view. Death in that sense is a tremendous release from monotony. It puts an end to all of total forgetting in a rhythmic process of on/off, on/off so you can begin all over again and never be bored. But the point is that if you can fantasize the idea of being nothing for always and always, what you are really saying is *after I'm dead the universe stops*, and what I'm saying is *it goes on* just as it did when you were born. You may think it incredible that you have more than one life, but isn't it incredible that you have this one? That's astonishing! And it can always happen again and again and again!

What I am saying then is just because you don't know how you manage to be conscious, how you manage to grow and shape your body, doesn't mean that you're not doing it. Equally, if you don't know how the universe shines the stars, constellates the constellations, or galactifies the galaxies—you don't know but that doesn't mean that you aren't doing it just the same way as you are breathing without knowing how you breathe.

If I say really and truly I am this whole universe, or this particular organism is an *I'ing* being done by the whole universe, then somebody could say to me, "Who the hell do you think you are? Are you God? Do you warm up the galaxies? *Canst' thou bind the sweet influences of the Pleiades or loosen the bonds of Orion?*" And I reply, "Who the hell do you think you are! Can you tell me how you grow your brain, how you shape your eyeballs, and how you manage to see? Well, if you can't tell me that, I can't tell you how I warm up the galaxy. Only I've located the center of myself at a deeper and more universal level than we are, in our culture, accustomed to do."

So then, if that universal energy is the real me, the real self which *I's* as different organisms in different spaces or places, and happening again and again at different times, we've got a marvelous system going in which you can be eternally surprised. The universe is really a system which keeps on surprising itself.

Many of us have an ambition, especially in an age of technological competence, to have everything under our control. This is a false ambition because you've only got to think for one moment what it would be like to really know and control everything. Supposing we had a supercolossal technology which could go to our wildest dreams of technological competence so that everything that is going to happen would be foreknown, predicted, and everything would be under our control. Why, it would be like making love to a plastic woman! There would be no surprise in it, no sudden answering touch as when we touch another human being. There comes out a response, something unexpected, and that's what we really want.

You can't experience the feeling you call self unless it's in contrast with the feeling of other. It's like known and unknown, light and dark, positive and negative. Other is necessary in order for you to feel self. Isn't that the arrangement you want? And, in the same way, couldn't you say the arrangement you want is not to remember? Memory is always, remember, a form of control: *I've got it in mind, I know your number, you're under control.* Eventually you want to release that control.

Now if you go on remembering and remembering and remembering, it's like writing on a piece of paper and going on writing and writing until there is no space left on the paper. Your memory is filled up and you need to wipe it clean so you can begin to write on it once more.

That's what death does for us: It wipes the slate clean and also, for looking at it from the point of view of population and the human organism on the planet, it keeps cleaning us out! A technology which would enable each one of us to be immortal would progressively crowd the planet with people having hopelessly crowded memories. They would be like people living in a house where they had accumulated so much property, so many books, so many vases, so many sets of knives and forks, so many tables and chairs, so many newspapers that there wouldn't be any room to move around.

To live we need space, and space is a kind of nothingness, and death is a kind of nothingness—it's all the same principle. And by putting blocks or spaces of nothingness, spaces of *space* in between spaces of *something*, we get life properly spaced out. The German word *lebensraum* means room for living, and that's what space gives us, and that's what death gives us.

Notice that in everything I've said about death I haven't brought in anything that I could call spookery. I haven't brought in any information about anything that you don't already know. I haven't invoked any mysterious knowledge about souls, memory of former lives, anything like that; I've just talked about it in terms that we already know. If you believe the idea that life beyond the grave is just wishful thinking, I'll grant that.

Let's assume that it is wishful thinking and when we are dead there just won't be anything. That'll be the end. Notice, first of all, that's the worst thing you've got to fear. Does it frighten you? Who's going to be afraid? Supposing it ends—no more problems.

But then you will see that this nothingness, if you've followed my argument, is something you'd *bounce* off from again just as you bounced in in the first place when you were born. You bounced out of nothingness. Nothingness is a kind of bounce because it implies that nothing implies something. You bounce back all new, all different, nothing to compare it with before, a refreshing experience.

You get this sense of nothingness, just like you've got the sense of nothing behind your eyes, very powerful frisky nothingness underlying your whole being. There's nothing in that nothing to be afraid of. With that sense you can come on like the rest of your life is gravy because you're already dead: You know you're going to die.

We say the only things certain are death and taxes. And the death of each one of us now is as certain as it would be if we were going to die five minutes from now. So where's your anxiety? Where's your hangup? Regard yourself as dead already so that you have nothing to lose. A Turkish proverb says, "He who sleeps on the floor will not fall out of bed." So in the same way is the person who regards himself as already dead.

Therefore, you are virtually nothing. A hundred years from now you will be a handful of dust, and that will be for real. All right now, act on that reality. And out of that ... nothing. You will suddenly surprise yourself: The more you know you are nothing the more you will amount to something.

# TIME

Photographs by Joseph McHugh

Time. What is time?

St. Augustine of Hippo when asked, "What is time?" said, "I know what it is, but when you ask me I don't." Yet it is absolutely fundamental to our life: "Time is money." "I don't have enough time." "Time flies." "Time drags."

I think we should question what time is, because of our ordinary common sense we think of it as a one-way motion from the past through the present and on into the future. That carries with it the impression that life moves from the past to the future in such a way that what happens now and what will happen is always the result of what has happened in the past. In other words, we seem to be driven along.

Once it was fashionable in psychology for people to speak of man's instincts, the instinct for survival, an instinct to make love, and so on. But nowadays that word has become unfashionable and psychologists tend instead to use the word *drive,* and to speak of the need for food as a drive, the need for survival or for sex as drives. That's a very significant word because it's brought out by people who feel driven. Personally, if I feel hungry I don't feel driven; if I feel lusty I don't feel driven; I don't say, "Oh, excuse me but I have to eat," or, "Excuse me but I need to fulfill my sexual urges." I say, "Hooray!" I identify myself with my drives. They are me, and I don't take a passive attitude towards them and apologize for them. So the whole idea of our being driven is connected with the idea of causality, of life moving under the power of the past. That is so ingrained in our common sense that it's very difficult to get rid of it. But I want to turn it round completely and say the past is the result of the present.

From one point of view that is very obvious. For example, let us suppose that this universe started with a big bang as some cosmologists believe. Now when that bang happened, it was the present, wasn't it? And so the universe began in what we will call a *now* moment, then it goes on doing its stuff. When any event that we now call past came into being, it came into being in the present and out of the present. That's one way of seeing it.

But before we get further involved in this, I want to draw your attention to a fallacy in the very commonsense idea of causality—events are caused by previous events from which they flow or necessarily result. To understand the fallacy of that idea, we have to begin by asking, "What do you mean by an event?" Let's take the event of a human being coming into the world. Now when does that event begin? Does it occur at the moment of parturition when the baby actually comes out of its mother? Or does the baby begin at the moment of conception? Or does a baby begin when it is a gleam in its father's eye? Or does a baby begin when the spermatozoa are generated in the father or the ova in the mother? Or could you say a baby begins when its father is born or when its mother is born? All these things can be thought of as beginnings, but we decide for purposes of legal registration that a life begins at the moment of parturition. And that is a purely arbitrary decision; it has validity only because we all agree about it.

114

Let me show you the same phenomenon in the dimension of space instead of the dimension of time. Let's ask, "How big is the sun?" Are we going to define the sun as limited by the extent of its fire? That's one possible definition. But we could equally well define the sphere of the sun by the extent of its light. And each of these would be reasonable choices. We have arbitrarily agreed to define the sun by the limit of its visible fire. But you see in these analogies that how big a thing is or how long an event is, is simply a matter of definition.

Therefore, when by the simple definition for purposes of discussion we have divided events into certain periods—the First World War began in 1914 and it ended in 1918 (actually, all those things which led up to the First World War started long before 1914, and the repercussions of that war continued long after 1918)—we sort of forget we do it. We have a puzzle, "How do events lead to each other?"

In reality there are no separate events. Life moves along like water, it's all connected as the source of the river is connected to the mouth and the ocean. All the events or things going on are like whirlpools in a stream. Today you see a whirlpool and tomorrow you see a whirlpool in the same place, but it isn't the same whirlpool because the water is changing every second.

What is happening is not really what we should call a whirlpool, but rather a whirlpooling. It is an *activity*, not a *thing*. And indeed every so-called thing can be called an event. We can call a house, *housing*, a mat, *matting*, and we could equally call a cat, a *catting*. So we could say, "The *catting* sat on the *matting*." And we would thereby have a world in which there were no things but only events. To give another illustration: A flame is something we say, "There is a flame on the candle." But it would be more correct to say, "There is a flaming on the candle," because a flame is a stream of hot gas.

117

Let's take another amusing example. *Fist* is a noun and fist looks like a thing, but what happens to the fist when I open my hand. I was fisting, now I'm handing, handing it to you. So every kind of so-called thing can be spoken of as an event and because events flow into each other, the fisting flows into the handing, we cannot say exactly where one ends and the other begins.

So, therefore, we do not need the idea of causality to explain how a prior event influences a following event. Consider it this way: Suppose I'm looking through a narrow slit in a fence, and a snake goes by. I've never seen a snake before, so it is mysterious. Through the fence I see first the snake's head, then I see a long trailing body, and then finally the tail. Then the snake turns around and goes back. Then I see first the head, and then after an interval the tail. Now if I call the head one event and the tail another, it will seem to me that the event *head* is the cause of the event *tail*. And the tail is the effect. But if I look at the whole snake I will see a head-tail snake and it would be simply absurd to say that the head of the snake is the cause of the tail, as if the snake came into being as a head first and then a tail. The snake comes into being out of its egg as a head-tail snake. And in exactly the same way all events are really one event. We are looking, when we talk about different events, at different sections or parts of one continuous happening.

Therefore, the idea of separate events, which have to be linked by a mysterious process called cause and effect, is completely unnecessary. But having thought that way, we think of present events as being caused by past events, and tend to regard ourselves as the *puppets* of the past, driven along by something that is always behind us.

118

It's very simple to overcome this impression. You begin with an experiment in meditation—approach the world through your ears. If you shut your eyes and make contact with reality purely with your ears, you will realize that the sounds you are hearing are all coming out of silence. It's curious isn't it because you hear all the realities, the sounds suddenly coming out of nothing. You don't see any reason for them to begin, they just appear and then they echo away through the corridors of the mind which we call memory.

Now if you open your eyes, it's a little harder to see this because unlike sound, the eyes sound static or rather, they see static. Everything looks still to your eyes, but you must understand that the world you are looking at is vibrating. All material things are vibrating and they are vibrating at you now in the same way as the sound was vibrating on your ears. In other words, the present world that you see is a vibration coming out of space just as the sound comes out of silence. It is coming out of nothing straight at you and echoing away into the past.

So the course of time is really very much like the course of a ship in the ocean. The ship leaves a wake behind it, and the wake fades out and tells us where the ship has been in just the same way as the past and our memory of the past tells us what we have done. But as we go back into the past, and we go back and back to prehistory and we use all kinds of instruments and scientific methods for detecting what happened, we eventually reach a point where all record of the past fades away in just the same way as the wake of a ship.

Now the important thing to remember in this illustration is that the wake doesn't drive the ship anymore than the tail wags the dog. The power, the source of the wake, is always in the ship itself which represents the present. You can't insist that the wake drives the ship. You can plot the course of the ship on graph paper and calculate a trend by seeing over what number of squares the ship has been doing its wiggling, and make predictions as to where it will go next. This would give you a trend as to where the ship is going and you might say, "Because we can plot the trend from the pattern which the ship has followed, we can tell where it is going and, therefore, we are inclined to think that where it has been will determine where it will go." But that is not actually the case. Where it has been is determined not by where it will go but where it is going. To put that more accurately, where it has been does not determine where it is going; where it is going determines where it has been.

If you insist that your present is the result of your past, you are like a person driving your car looking always in the rear-view mirror. You are not, as it were, open to the future, you are always looking back over your shoulder to find out what you ought to do. And this is something absolutely characteristic of us and this is why human beings find it difficult to learn and difficult to adapt themselves to new situations. Because we are always looking for precedents, for authority from the past for what we are supposed to do now, that gives us the impression the past is all-important and is the determinative factor in our behavior.

It isn't anything of the kind. The life, the creation, comes out of you now. In other words, don't look for the creation back here at the beginning of where the wake fades out. Don't look for the creation of the universe at some very far-distant point in time behind us. The creation of the universe is now in this present instant. This is where it all begins! And it trails away from here and eventually vanishes.

122

Now of course we have a method of passing the buck in all matters of responsibility by saying, "Well, the past is responsible for me." For instance, when dealing with a difficult child, we are apt to say, "Well, bang him about, beat him up, and maybe he'll change." But then we say, "No, that's not fair to the child to beat him up, because it was his parents' fault; they didn't bring him up properly." And so then we say, "Well, punish the parents." But the parents say, "Well, excuse me, but our parents were neurotic, too, and they brought us up badly so we couldn't help what we did." And since the grandparents are dead we can't get at them, and if we could we would pass the whole blame back to Adam and Eve. We would say, "They started all this mess." But then Eve would say, "No, the serpent tempted me and I did eat." Then it was the serpent's fault!

When God asked Eve, "Didst thou eat the fruit of the tree whereof I told thee thou shouldst not eat?" she said, "Oh, but the serpent tempted me and I did eat." And God looked at the serpent, and the serpent didn't make any excuse. He probably winked—because the serpent, being an angel, was wise enough to know where the present begins.

So you see, if you insist on being moved, being determined by the past, that's your game. But the fact of the matter is *it all starts right now*. But we like to establish a connectivity with the past because that gives other people the impression that we're sane. People ask, for example, why you do something. Now that's a ridiculous question. A child finds out that to irritate its parents it can always put the word *why* after any answer to a question. "Why does the sun shine?" and he gets an astronomical explanation, "Well, why does nuclear heat generate in star bodies?" "Oh, because it reaches a critical mass." "Well, why does it reach a critical mass?" And you can go on and on and on asking why until papa says, "Oh, shut up and suck your lollipop."

The question "why," because it can be asked interminably, never leads to any interesting answers. If you ask me then *why* am I proposing this, I could say, "Well, I'm making a living this way, or I have a message I want to get across to you." But that's not the reason. I am talking for the same reason that birds sing and the stars shine. I dig it. Why do I dig it? I could go on answering all sorts of questions about human motivation and psychology, but they wouldn't explain a thing, because explaining things by the past is really a refusal to explain them at all. All you're doing is postponing the explanation. You're putting it back and back and back and that explains nothing.

What does explain things is the present. Why do you do it now? Now this is a slight cheat because that doesn't explain it either, because what happens now, just as the sound comes out of silence, all this comes out of nowhere. All life suddenly emerges out of space—Bang! Right now!

And to ask again why does it happen is an unprofitable question because the interesting thing is not why but what. What happens? Not, why does it happen? I can say, "Well, I am doing this now because I did that then," and so I am producing for you a continuous line of thought, but actually I am doing it backwards. I'm doing it always from now and connecting up what I do now with what I did so that you can see a consistent story.

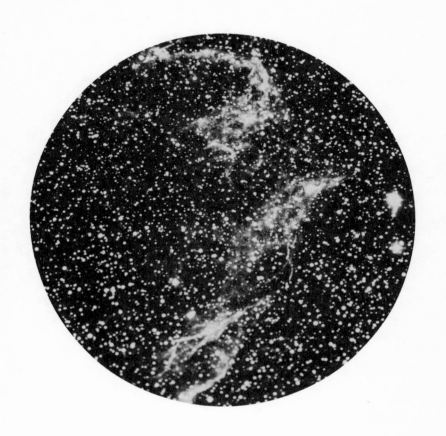

Now another interesting thing about this is that I can show you how the present changes the past. Let's take for example the order of words. Now words are strung out in a line just like we think events in time are strung out in a line and I can change a past word by a future word. If I say (taking a line from the poet Thomas Hood), "They went and told the sexton, and the sexton tolled the bell." You don't know what the first *told* means until you get the sexton; you don't know what the second *tolled* means until you get to the word *bell*. And so the later event changes the meaning of the former. Or you can say for example, "The bark of the tree," and the word *bark* has a certain meaning. Then I say, "The bark of the dog," and the later word has changed the meaning of the former one.

And so, in this way, when we write history we find that writing history is really an art. The historian keeps putting a fresh interpretation on past events and in that sense he is changing it. He is changing their meaning just like we were changing the meaning of a former word by a later word by saying, "They went and told the sexton and the sexton tolled the bell."

In this way you can experience a curious liberation from what the Hindus and the Buddhists call *karma*. The word *karma* in Sanskrit actually means doing, action. *Karma* comes from the root *kri* which simply means *to do*. When something happens to me, an accident or an illness, a Buddhist or a Hindu will say, "Well, it was your karma." In other words, you had done something in the past and you reap the unfortunate consequence in a later time. Now that's not the real meaning of karma. Karma does not mean cause and effect. It simply means doing. In other words, you are doing what is happening to you. And that, of course, depends upon how you define the word *you*. For example, consider breathing; am I doing it or is it happening to me? I am growing my hair; am I doing it or is it happening to me? You can look at it either way. I am being sick, or I am being destroyed in an accident—if I define myself as the whole field of events, the organism-environment field which is the real me, then all the things that happen to me may be called my doing. And that is the real sense of karma.

But when we speak about freedom from karma, freedom from being the puppet of the past, that simply involves a change in our thinking. It involves getting rid of the habit of thought whereby we define ourselves as the result of what has gone before. We instead get into the more plausible, more reasonable habit of thought in which we don't define ourselves in terms of what we've done before but in terms of what we're doing now. And that is liberation from the ridiculous situation of being a dog wagged by its tail.

THE
NATURE
of MAN

The Tibetans use a wooden cylinder mounted on an axis for saying prayers. They sit comfortably and spin it around with little effort and their prayers are said for them by this prayer wheel and they relax for the few minutes it takes. Westerners think this is a superstition, a meaningless heathen ritual. It doesn't require any great effort; it's nothing like work or duty; and there's no expression of humility or unworthiness. Any child would enjoy doing it. It's curious; it's fascinating.

I happen to like archery—not for killing things, but as a sport. What I like most of all is to set an arrow free like a bird. It climbs high into the sky, then suddenly turns and drops.

What is it that fascinates us about that? We are delighted by it because it's not useful. It doesn't really achieve anything that we would call purposive work. It is simply what we call play. But in our culture we make an extremely rigid division between work and play. You are supposed to work in order to earn enough money to give you sufficient leisure time for something entirely different called *having fun* or play.

This is a most ridiculous division. Everything that we do, however tough it is, however strenuous, can be turned into the same kind of play as shooting an arrow into the sky or spinning a prayer wheel. Let's, for example, take the situation that I ran into a little while ago: I was in the New York subway at 59th Street near Columbus Circle, and I wanted to get my shoes shined. (Actually, I don't wear shoes except on the East Coast. There one dresses respectably. On the West Coast I wear Indian moccasins because it's the only comfortable shoe I can wear.) I found a place to get my shoes shined and there was a Black who was making shoe-shining a real art. He used his cloth to beat out a rhythm. He had just the same fascination in shining shoes as one has in spinning a prayer wheel or shooting an arrow. Imagine if you were a bus driver. A bus driver is ordinarily considered a totally harassed person. He's got to watch out for all the laws, all the competing traffic, the people coming on board giving their fares, and he has to make change. And if he has it in his head that this is work, it will be hell. But let's suppose he has a different thing in his head. Suppose he has the idea that moving this enormous conveyance through complicated traffic is a very, very subtle game; he has the very same feeling about it that you might have if you were playing the guitar or dancing. And so he goes through that traffic avoiding this and avoiding that and taking fares, and he makes a music of the whole thing. Well, he's not going to be tired out at the end of the day. He's going to be full of energy when he gets through with his job.

134

Suppose you're condemned to be a housewife, which is the most lowly of all occupations, and you have to clean up. There are only four fundamental philosophical questions. The first is "Who started it?" The second is "Are we going to make it?" The third is "Where are we going to put it?" And the fourth is "Who's going to clean up?" And this, the cleaning up, is the lowliest of all occupations, the housewife who washes the dishes and the garbage collector who takes away the stuff. Supposing the housewife about to clean up approaches washing dishes in an entirely different spirit. And don't think I'm some sort of male chauvinist who's trying to talk women into the idea of staying in their place. I'm perfectly willing to wash dishes too, because the art of washing dishes is that you only have to wash one at a time. If you're doing it day after day you have in your mind's eye an enormous stack of filthy dishes which you have washed in years past and an enormous stack of filthy dishes which you will wash in future years. But if you bring your mind to the state of reality which is only now, this is where we are, you only have to wash one dish. It's the only dish you'll ever have to wash. You ignore all the rest, because in reality there is no past and there is no future. There is just now. So you wash this one. And instead of thinking, "Have I got it really clean as my mother taught?", you turn the cleaning movement into a dance, you swing that plate around, you let the rinsing water run over it, and you put it in the rack—you get a rhythm going.

When I was a little boy and went to school in England I had to learn the piano. They called it playing the piano, but actually they said, "You *must* play." We had, also in England, compulsory games. They used to post notices on the bulletin board in the school that said, "This afternoon everyone will go for a run." And if you didn't go for a run and it was found out, you were flogged! So everybody hated going for a run because they were under compulsion to play. It's like the whole game of life we're involved in. It's only a game, but everybody has got to belong.

137

I remember one day I was out on a run and I was trying to enjoy myself, running on the balls of my feet, dancing along. A fellow came up behind me who was running on his heels. He was jogging, and going clunk-clunk-clunk-clunk-clunk-clunk, and I said to him, "What's the matter with you? You're running on your heels and you are jarring your whole body all the way through." He shrugged, stuck to it, and became the champion long-distance runner of the school. But he didn't enjoy it! It was work! All he enjoyed was the suffering that he endured. It made him feel he had really contributed to the human race by suffering so much. He identified his existence and his worth with his suffering. Now really great runners dance when they run. They don't necessarily follow a straight course; they may weave. A great example of this occurred in 1970 in the World Cup Championship of soccer. The winning team from Brazil, which consisted mostly of Blacks, played soccer in a most extraordinary way: They played it like basketball; they danced. The way we learned soccer in school when I was a boy was very, very formal and orderly, and we didn't really enjoy it. But these fellows were bounding balls off their shoulders, off every muscle. and they had astonishing team-work, and at the same time they were dancing. The sports writer in *The London Times* said, "They danced their way to victory." So the point is that you can do everything you have to do in this spirit. Don't make a distinction between work and play, and don't imagine for one minute that you've got to be serious about it.

Let's take, for example, the rest of the world rather than ourselves. Think for a moment: What are plants doing? What are plants all about? They serve human beings by being decorative, but what is *it* from its own point of view? It's using up air; it's using up energy. It's really not doing anything except being ornamental. And yet here's this whole vegetable world, cactus plants, trees, roses, tulips, and edible vegetables, like cabbages, celery, lettuce—they're all doing this dance. And what's it all about? Why are they doing it? Well, we say, one must live. It's necessary to survive. You know you really must go on. It's your duty. It's your duty to your children. If you bring up your children that way and tell them they should be grateful because you are doing your duty towards them, they will learn to bring up their children in the same way—and everybody will be depressed. There really is no necessity to go on living. It's part of Western philosophy, this drive to survive. We must go on living because some big daddy said to us, "You've got to go on living, see? And you'd better make it or else!" Well, the fear of death is completely absurd. Because if you're dead you've got nothing to worry about! This plant, I'm quite sure, doesn't say to itself, "You ought to go on living." You've got, just as it has, an instinct to survive which is something other than yourself and which you have to obey.

I don't think of my own instincts as *drives*, which is the proper psychological term for them nowadays. I think of my instincts as myself. I don't say, "Excuse me, but I have an unfortunate desire to reproduce myself; would you please accommodate me." I don't say, "Excuse me, but I have to eat: it's absolutely necessary that I eat." I say, "Hooray! I am this desire to make love, and I am this desire to eat." It's not something else that pushes me around; it's me. It doesn't have to go on. If it were to stop, if I were to die, that would be another scene; that would be a different form of the dance.

141

If I'm in pain, people say don't scream, don't cry. But
screaming or crying is a perfectly natural reaction to pain.
When a baby is first born they cut the umbilical cord and
someone smacks it on the bottom and the baby cries. That's
the first thing in the world. There is in Zen Buddhism a *koan*
that says when the Buddha was born he suddenly stood up
and announced, "Above the heavens and below the heavens,
I alone am the world-honored one." Well, everybody would
say that's an extremely proud thing to say. So they give this
to students of Buddhism as a problem: How could it be that
the Buddha as a little baby was so proud as to make this
pompous statement when he was born? And if you
understand the problem correctly, you cry like a newborn
baby. Because that is the perfectly natural response to the
painful event of being born into this world. But thereafter we
say, "Baby, don't you cry! Shut up!" And therefore we stamp
out in human beings their natural release from the problem of
pain. If you're in pain, cry. And if you can't do that, then
pain is your problem. But if you *can* cry, if you can let go in
that way, pain is no problem. And if you get the shudders at
death, the idea of death, the idea of not being here anymore,
just get those shudders and dig them. Isn't it curious? You
really get the shivers of delight!

So all these emotions that we have, the emotions of
uptightness, dread, shivers, horrors, can be intepreted in
other ways. But we interpret them in a negative way so long
as we are under the sense that you absolutely must go on
living. Now, you see, living is something spontaneous. In
Chinese the word for nature is *ch'i lan*, which means that
which happens of itself, not under any control of an outside
entity. And they feel that all the world is happening of itself;
it's spontaneous. And you stop this spontaneous flowering of
nature cold if you tell it it must do it. It's like saying to
someone, "You must love me." Well it's ridiculous. If I were
to ask my wife, "Darling, do you really love me?" and, she
says, "I'm trying my best to do so," that's not the answer I
want. I want her to say, "I can't help loving you. I love you
so much I could eat you." And that's what the plant feels in
growing. It doesn't feel it must grow; it's not under orders. It
does this spontaneously so that when you try to command
this spontaneous process, you stop it.

There is a belief in India that if you think of a monkey while
you're taking medicine it won't work. Next time you take
your vitamins or pills try not to think of a monkey. You will
completely tie up the spontaneous process, and it won't
work. So all the things that we say to our children, like, "You
must have a bowel movement every day after breakfast";
"Try, darling, to go to sleep"; "Stop pouting; take that look
off your face"; "Oh, you're blushing." They all make you feel
guilty. All those things are attempts to say this one thing,
"Darling little child, you are required to do what will be
acceptable only if you do it voluntarily." On this account,
everybody is completely mixed up because we are trying to
force genuine behavior. We all admire artists; we say they're
unselfconscious, they're so natural, they seem to dance or
paint or talk or play the piano so effortlessly. Of course, a lot
of work has gone into it, but if you are a great artist your
periods of practice will not be effective unless they are a
pleasure for you. You have to come to the point where going
over it again and again is a dance.

145

One of my friends is a great Hindu musician who has the most extraordinary technique of playing an instrument called the sarod. It's like an extremely sophisticated Hindu guitar. His name is Ali Akbar Khan and he is generally acknowledged to be the leading master of Northern Indian music. He once told me that the comprehension of music is in understanding one note. He can sit for hours and hours working on only one note at a time. He gets into that note and listens. He really listens, gets into the sound. It simply doesn't matter that it takes a long time, that he has to do this for many hours, because he's completely absorbed in listening to the sound he is now making. He's going with that vibration, as when you might chant like they do in yoga, "OM." You can chant for hours and be absolutely fascinated by the vibration in the same way as I am fascinated shooting an arrow into the sky. Now what is it? This is the real secret of life—to be completely engaged with what you are doing in the here and now. And instead of calling it work, realize that it is play.

In Hindu philosophy the whole creation is regarded as the *Vishnu Lila*, the Play of Vishnu. Lila means dance or play. Also, in Hindu philosophy, they call the world an illusion; and in Latin the root of the word illusion is *ludere*, to play. All that is going on, the spinning of the prayer wheel, the pattern in which the flower grows, is just the living. And if you take it seriously and say, "Are you doing anything useful?" Useful for what? Useful for going on? But if you have to be useful for going on, going on becomes a drag, survival becomes a sweat, and it's not worth it. And if you teach this to your children, they'll imitate you. They'll treat survival as an ordeal which they have to undergo. They have to keep going on and they'll teach their children to do it, and the whole continuation of the human race will be a drag which is in fact what it has become because of this attitude. And this is the reason we have invented the atomic bomb and are preparing to commit suicide. We think we must happen and, to the degree to which we think we must happen, we hate it, and are going to bring it to an end, stop it.

146

So I sincerely suggest (I'm talking with you; I'm not preaching) as G. K. Chesterton once said, "The angels fly because they take themselves lightly. How much more so than he-she who is Lord of the Angels.  The whole world is three for a penny, three for a pound, it's love that makes the world go round." Or in the words of Dante:

> "That my own wings were not to flutter
>   Were not for such a flight
>   Except that smiting through the mind of me
>   There came fulfillment in a flash of light.
>   That my volition now and my desires
>   Were moved like wheel-revolving evenly
>   By love that moves the sun in starry sky.

Thither my own wings could not carry me,
  But that a flash my understanding clove,
  Whence its desire came to it suddenly.

High fantasy lost power and here broke off;
  Yet, as a wheel moves smoothly, free from jars,
  My will and my desire were turned by love,

The love that moves the sun and the other stars."

End of Canto XXXIII   Paradise

When I was a boy in London, I used to love to visit the British Museum. In the neighborhood of the museum were a number of old shops, some of them dating from the end of the 18th century. The inscription over one shop window said they sold philosophical instruments. I couldn't for the life of me figure out what philosophical instruments could be. I thought philosophers were people who simply sat thinking and wouldn't have any need for any special instruments. But when I went up to this shop I found that what they had in the window were telescopes, slide rules, chronometers, and all sorts of what we could now call scientific instruments, because the original name for science was *natural philosophy*. A philosopher is a person who is curious about everything. He's not only curious about theoretical matters, but he's also curious about what we should now call practical matters. I regard myself as a philosopher in exactly that sense. Aside from being interested in changed states of consciousness, the problems of death, problems of time and space, and the practice of meditation, I am also interested in what you would call down-to-earth things, such as food, clothing, housing, problems of ecology and population, because all of this is part of natural curiosity or philosophy.

One thing that tells us a great deal about our society, about our nature, is clothing. I am now arrayed in what has become the standard official man's dress for the whole world—the business suit. Derived from England, popularized in America, adopted by the Japanese, the Indonesians, the Indians, the Persians, the Arabs, everybody on the face of the earth is now tending to go around dressed like this in a peculiar form of clothing derived from military uniforms. You will notice that it has buttons on the sleeve. Now what do you suppose those are for? They don't fasten to anything.

Originally, on the uniforms from which these coats were derived, there was a whole row of buttons all the way up, and they were on military uniforms or uniforms worn by servitors to prevent them from wiping their noses on their sleeves. And then it has these curious lapels, and goodness knows what purpose they served. Sometimes people turn them up to try to protect themselves from the rain, but they are not really very effective. And then you have to wear a shirt and strangle yourself with a necktie. Also, you have to wear pants, British trousers, which is a most devastating garment for men. Trousers are worn by Chinese women; Chinese men in the old times, before the era of Mao Tse Tung, wore skirts. Trousers are a garment suitable for shapely women—they are not at all suitable for men because they are castrative and extremely uncomfortable, especially if you want to sit on the floor. To wear a business suit and be comfortable you invariably have to sit on a chair. If you don't your trousers will become baggy at the knees. Also, the coat and shirt are very difficult to fold if you have to put them in a suitcase. The problem of the business suit is that it is made to fit the contours of the human body. It has to be tailored to show off your form, which is all very well if you have a slim form! Another problem is how do you keep the trousers suspended? I still wear a belt, but the time is going to come when I have to wear suspenders, a kind of block-and-tackle contraption which is another and further inconvenience. It just astonishes me that all over the world men are putting up with this drab, funeral uniform, looking like undertakers and ministers when they could be much more comfortable. I could be just as comfortable, just as proper, just as demure, by wearing a Japanese kimono, which is worn not so much in modern times as 50 years ago by all Japanese gentlemen.

The kimono is one of the most extraordinary garments ever made. To begin with, it is completely comfortable. You feel absolutely relaxed underneath it; nothing is restricting you anywhere. It has tremendously capacious sleeves which are immense pockets into which you can put anything you want—your wallet, your pipe and tobacco or cigarettes, and money, anything you want. With a kimono it's quite proper to carry a fan, and when the weather is too hot you can cool yourself off. There is an outer garment, the *haori*, which is actually a coat for cooler weather and for rather proper occasions. You can take the haori off and just wear what's underneath and have the same thing as before with the big sleeves and enormous pockets. There is a peculiar thing about a kimono, that is that it is entirely cut from rectangular pieces of cloth. The cloth has not been shaped to fit the human body. Cloth is naturally rectangular because of its being woven material with a perpendicular warp and horizontal woof.

Now, in designing this form of clothes we do not
alter the rectangular nature of the cloth. We do not
attempt to shape it in any other way to force it to fit the
curves of the human body. But if we honor the nature of
cloth in that way and respect its nature, curiously enough it
respects our nature. Because if you hang rectangular cloth
upon you it falls in folds which give you a kind of natural
dignity. When you shape the cloth to you, you begin to look
more and more like a monkey. But when you allow the cloth
to hang upon you and follow its own nature, you look more
and more like a prince. This is the essential principle of
Japanese clothing. However, the Japanese have been
abandoning this clothing. I asked one of them why and the
first thing he said was, "Well, it's impossible to run for a bus
in a kimono." And that's perfectly true! You cannot run in
this garment; you have to walk at a dignified pace, and I
think that is very good for us. I don't think any
self-respecting person should ever run for a bus; we need
above all for things to slow down and get ourselves to amble
through life instead of rush through it. And, therefore, I
consider that this garment, commonly worn by men, would
have an enormously beneficent effect on American
civilization. We would be much more comfortable, much
more at ease, much more dignified. I wear one all the time.

The style of kimono worn for normal purposes is called the *yukata*. It is a cotton kimono which the Japanese businessman would don when he gets home. But, first, he takes a very hot bath in an enormous tub where practically the whole family can sit together. It's a wonderful institution. It's the first thing you do when you get home from work. You don't wash in the tub; you wash by taking a bucket and sloshing yourself with water from the tub, soap yourself, and rinse off; and then you sit in the bath and steam rises all about you and you smoke cigarettes and chat with all the family. And that's the greatest kind of bath in all the world. After the bath you get into your yakata. It is perfectly permissible to go out strolling in the streets in the evening dressed in this type of kimono. The warm-weather yukata is made of cotton, and the cold-weather yukata, called a *penzen*, is made of padded silk. You can wear your kimono with a sash called an *obi*. Men's obi are made with tie-dye ornamentations on the end, and women's obi are much more stiff and made of very, very heavy silk—not nearly as comfortable to wear. This is an absolutely perfectly relaxed dress for men. Since I am a writer and do most of my work at home, I wear one of these most all of the time because it is not constricting, and because of the extreme convenience of the pockets. When you notice how the sash fastens into an elegant bow in the back you may think that, along with the absence of pants, it is effeminate. But men, especially in America and England, are terribly uptight about coming on in a way they suppose to be feminine. They say, "Skirts are women, sissy stuff!" But if you are biologically male you don't need to prove that you are. It is so strange to me how an enormous number of men don't seem to be able to realize that they are men unless they can in some way come on with tremendous energy, very strong, that shows off their manhood. But if you're a real man you don't need to show that at all. All you need to do to find out if you are a real man is ask a woman.

There is another garment worth considering and this is the ancient Greek *chlamys*. It is a long, linen garment that has come down to us in modern times through the Roman Catholic Church in the form of an *alb*, which a priest wears at Mass over his ordinary suit. He takes off his coat and puts on a long, heavy, black garment called a cassock, and then he puts this extra suit of clothes, the alb, over it. But any sensible priest in celebrating Mass would take off all his clothes and simply wear his underpants and his chlamys, or alb. Also, there is a hood which can be pulled over your head and makes a comfortable thing around the neck—it catches the sweat. It's called an *amice*. So this is what men in our Western world commonly wore back about 400 B.C. and afterwards in Greece. The *toga* was worn in Rome, a somewhat more inconvenient garment because you had to throw it over you and all the folds of cloth were always dropping down and falling off. But the chlamys is extremely comfortable and very convenient. Along with the alb, or chlamys, a priest of the Catholic Church when celebrating Mass will wear over this garment called a *chasuble* in English, *casubla* in Latin. And the word *casubla* means a little house or a tent; it is much like a poncho, a garment which you could tie to a pole, spread out, put stones on it and rest under during the night to keep the rain off you. You could make a chasuble, a poncho, simply by taking a perfectly square piece of cloth, hem it, cut a slit in it, and then you have a tent. It goes easily over your head, and without any tailoring or fitting you at once have a very dignified and becoming garment. They are of enormous use, you can wear them with anything, they keep you beautifully warm especially if you make them out of some heavy material. I have one that is made of camel's hair. And once when I wore it I was stopped in a bar by an Irishman who said, "Where have I seen that before?" "Well," I said, "you saw a priest wearing it at Mass," which he thought was very funny. But this essential poncho gives great freedom of movement; your hands are free and it's very warm and you can wear it over loosefitting clothes and be extremely comfortable, not castrated, and at your ease.

161

Of all the garments we will consider, the most outlandish is the Philippine *sarong*. My Japanese friend said you can't run for a bus in a kimono. All right, you could sure run for a bus in a Philippine sarong, because it gives you complete freedom for your legs. It is essentially a divided skirt, very floppy, made of cotton, which wraps around and tucks in at the waist and can be secured with a safety pin. Over it you simply wear a colorful shirt. The sarong, with variations, is worn all over South Asia, but the Philippine design with the divide is the most comfortable, the most elastic I have ever discovered, and I do not know any more comfortable form of dress in the world. You can make it from any material, out of worsted in order to be warm in cold weather and have a completely comfortable and reasonably dignified form of clothing.

Well, now, what is our problem? What's the problem with Western man and even Western woman that they dress so damned uncomfortable. I've thought about this a great deal because it comes down to some fundamental philosophical matters. One of them is this: When people get up in the morning they put on a bathrobe, and after a little time goes by they feel slightly guilty. Why do they feel slightly guilty? Because, when you have got loose-fitting clothes on, you may have a slight suspicion that you don't really exist. In other words, you are not strapped in. All people of action wear big belts and boots—things that clutch you tightly. And then you feel, because of the pressure on your skin, that you are really there. Now this is a very serious mistake, especially for soldiers. I maintain that the German army lost two world wars because of the goosestep, because of military pomp and swagger, because of such things as brass bands and close-order drill. Because a really effective army should be invisible and inaudible. But you cannot get men who are on the machismo kick, who have to prove they are men, to be invisible and inaudible. A truly effective army, an army of guerrillas, should dress with complete comfort, complete practicality, and no kind of tieing themselves together in knots so the pressure will assure you that you are there. That's like sleeping on a bed of nails! But a great many people in our culture don't feel that they are really alive unless in some way they are uncomfortable or suffering. And the reason is that we have a profound, built-in sense of guilt about our existence because we feel that we don't really belong to the universe.

There is a wonderful story about a Japanese mystic, a kind of wandering holy man who one night stopped in a Buddhist temple for shelter. He went up to the high altar and there were all these kneeling cushions which the priests use for celebrating the service. He arranged them all and made a comfortable bed and went to sleep. Early in the morning the priests came in to celebrate the service and saw this apparent bum lying on all the cushions in front of the altar. "Hey," they said, "what are you doing here? Such disrespectful conduct in front of the altar!" And the holy man looked up at them and said, "Oh? You must be a stranger here; you cannot belong to the family." And so, likewise, in an Italian church, little children were running in and out of the pews ducking back and forth while their mother was offering candles at the shrine of Saint Anthony. Two American spinsters from New England were viewing the church and were very shocked at the way these children were playing. They went over and touched the mother on the shoulder and said, "Don't you think these children should be controlled?" "Well," she said, "it is their Father's house; can't they play here?"

But that's a most curious thing, isn't it? Our clothing is undertaker clothing, military clothing, ministerial clothing. For in our culture we *cultivate* an uptight attitude: "Hold yourself in! Restrain yourself!" But in doing this we are constantly at war with ourselves. Our society tells us that we are a nasty little animal that has to be controlled and beaten into submission, and, on the other hand, we are a rational soul which is a sort of higher self supposed to take control of the lower self. And for this reason we are always at cross purposes with ourselves. Freud, for example, distinguished between the pleasure principle, which he located in the genital region, and the reality principle, which he located in the cortical region of the brain, so that there is a distance between these two centers. Because they are not in the same place, for some reason or other it seems there always has to be a fight between them. In a flower, the mind and sex organ are in the same place, so it doesn't have that conflict. But in the human being they are divided (at least, we think they are divided) simply because they are at a distance from each other in space.

But they are not really divided at all. They look different. The head looks very different from the genitals, but in the same way bees look very different from flowers. One flies in the air and buzzes, and the other is rooted in the ground and colorfully perfumes the environment so the bee is attracted to it. But these two very different looking things are in fact one single organism: If there are no bees there are no flowers; if there are no flowers there are no bees. They come together, as the Chinese say, to arise mutually. In the same way, when you were born, your head and your genitals arose mutually. They came in together; they are not really separate from each other.

Therefore, this idea that living an ordered life consists in controlling yourself, is doing nothing but creating a conflict and a disturbance inside yourself. Imagine what it would be like if you had to control the movement of your right hand with your left hand. If I want to pick up a cigar with my right hand, my left hand would come over and grab it and direct it to the object, close the fingers around it, and carry it to my mouth. Wouldn't that be absurd? But that is what we are doing all the time when we divide ourselves into two parts, the spiritual and the material, the angelic and the animal, and the rational and irrational. We are constantly holding clubs over ourselves. That is one of the reasons why, when you get up in the morning and put on your bathrobe, after awhile you begin to feel guilty. You feel you should be, as we say, dressed and in your right mind, so that you can go out and be a person of action. So you can *feel* yourself meeting your obligations, doing your duty.

Every day in the urban areas millions of people are literally wearing themselves out, tearing their nerves to distraction, by going along the freeways in a car, fouling the atmosphere, to do their work. That wonderful work which is completely divorced, quite separate, from their play. Now this is one of the great insanities of our civilization. Every sensible person should get paid for playing. If you don't get paid for playing something is wrong with you—you haven't learned the art of life. But we have got this idea that work is one thing and play is another, therefore we have work-clothes—the business suit—and we have play-clothes. And I suggest that one of the most important things is to get our heads together with our genitals, our genitals together with our heads, and our work together with our play, and make our life a pleasure—unified and one.

THE
COSMIC
DRAMA

Photographs by Mike Powers and Maria Demarest

I want you to think of the curious sensation of *nothing* that lies behind ourselves. Think of the blank space behind the eyes, about the silence out of which all sound comes, and about empty space, out of which all the stars appear. I liken this curious emptiness behind everything to God, an imageless, non-idolatrous God of which we can have no conception at all. Basically, when you really get down to it, that emptiness is yourself.

Now it sounds very odd in our civilization to say, "Therefore, I am God," or for that matter, "You are God." But this is exactly what Jesus Christ felt. And he was crucified for it, because in his culture God was conceived as the royal monarch of the universe, and anybody who got up and said, "Well, I am God," was blasphemous. He was subversive. He was claiming to be, if not the boss himself, at least the boss' son, and that was a put-down for everybody else. But Jesus had to say it that way because, in his culture, they did not have, as the Hindus have, the idea that everybody, not only human beings, but animals and plants, all sentient beings whatsoever, are God in disguise.

Now, let me try to explain this a little more clearly. I cannot help thinking of myself as identical with, continuous with, one with the whole energy that expresses itself as this universe. If the universe is made up of stars, a star is a center from which energy flows. In other words there's the middle, and all the rays come out from it. And so I feel that, as the image of the whole thing, all energy is a center from which rays come out and, therefore, each one of us is an expression of what is basically the whole thing.

In the Jewish, Christian, and Islamic religions we think of God not only as a monarch but as the maker of the world, and, as a result of that, we look upon the world as an artifact, a sort of machine, created by a great engineer. There's a different conception in India, where the world is not seen as an artifact, but as a drama. And therefore God is not the maker and architect of the universe but the actor of it, and is playing all the parts at once, and this connects up with the idea of each one of us as persons, because a person is a mask, from the Latin *persona*, the mask worn by the actors in Greco-Roman drama. So this is an entirely different conception of the world, and as I think I shall be able to show you, it makes an amazing amount of sense.

So we start with the premise that you are God, and you don't know how you grow your body, how you make your nervous system work, how you manage to emerge in this environment of nature. All this is unknown to you, the you that is not you, the you that is not the ego. This is God—that is to say, not the cosmic boss, but the fundamental ground of being, the reality that always was, is, and will be, that lies at the basis of reality. That's you.

174

Now, let's go into a more mythological kind of imagery. Suppose you're God. Suppose you have all time, eternity, and all power at your disposal. What would you do? I believe you would say to yourself after awhile, "Man, get lost." It's like asking another question which amounts to supposing you were given the power to dream any dream you wanted to dream every night. Naturally, you could dream any span of time—you could dream seventy-five years of time in one night, a hundred years of time in one night, a thousand years of time in one night—and it could be anything you wanted—because you make up your mind before you go to sleep, "Tonight I'm going to dream of so-and-so." Naturally, you would start out by fulfilling all your wishes. You would have all the pleasures you could imagine, the most marvelous meals, the most entrancing love affairs, the most romantic journeys, you could listen to music such as no mortal has heard, and see landscapes beyond your wildest dreams.

And for several nights, oh, maybe for a whole month of nights, you would go on that way, having a wonderful time. But then, after a while, you would begin to think, "Well, I've seen quite a bit, let's spice it up, let's have a little adventure." And you would dream of yourself being threatened by all sorts of dangers. You would rescue princesses from dragons, you would perhaps engage in notable battles, you would be a hero. And then as time went on, you would dare yourself to do more and more outrageous things, and at some point in the game you would say, "Tonight I am going to dream in such a way that I don't know that I'm dreaming," and by so doing you would take the experience of the drama for complete reality. What a shock when you woke up! You could really scare yourself!

And then on successive nights you might dare yourself to experience even more extraordinary things just for the contrast when you woke up. You could, for example, dream yourself in situations of extreme poverty, disease, agony. You could, as it were, live the essence of suffering to its most intense point, and then, suddenly, wake up and find it was after all nothing but a dream and everything's perfectly O.K.

Well, how do you know that's not what you're doing already. You, reading, sitting there with all your problems, with all your whole complicated life situations, it may just be the very dream you decided to get into. If you don't like it, what fun it'll be when you wake up!

This is the essence of drama. In drama, all the people who see it know it's only a play. The proscenium arch, the cinema screen tells us, "Well, this is an illusion, it is not for real." In other words, they are going to act their parts so convincingly that they're going to have us sitting on the edge of our seats in anxiety, they're going to make us laugh, they're going to make us cry, they're going to make us feel horror. And all the time, in the back of our minds we have what Germans call *hintergedanken* which is a thought way, way, way in the back of our minds, that we're hardly aware of but really know all the time. In the theater, we have a hintergedanken that it's only a play. But the mastery of the actors is going to almost convince us that it's real.

And, so, imagine a situation in which you have the best of all possible actors, namely God, and the best of all possible audiences ready to be taken in and convinced that it's real, namely God, and that you are all many, many masks which the basic consciousness, the basic mind of the universe, is assuming. To use a verse from G. K. Chesterton:

*But now a great thing in the street*
*Seems any human nod*
*Where shift in strange democracy*
*The million masks of God.*

It is like the mask of Vishnu, the preserver of the universe, a multiple mask which illustrates the fact that the one who looks out of my eyes and out of everyone's eyes is the same center. So, when I look at another human being, and I look straight into their eyes, I don't like doing that, there's something embarrassing about looking into someone's eyes too closely. Don't look at me that closely because I might give myself away! You might find out who I really am! And what do you suppose that would be? Do you suppose that another person who looks deeply into your eyes will read all the things you're ashamed of, all your faults, all the things you are guilty of? Or is there some deeper secret than that?

The eyes are our most sensitive organ, and when you look and look and look into another person's eyes you are looking at the most beautiful jewels in the universe. And if you look down beyond that surface beauty, it's the most beautiful jewel in the universe, because that's the universe looking at you. We are the eyes of the cosmos. So that in a way, when you look deeply into somebody's eyes, you're looking deep into yourself, and the other person is looking deeply into the same self, which many-eyed, as the mask of Vishnu is many-faced, is looking out everywhere, one energy playing myriads of different parts. Why?

181

It's perfectly obvious, because if you were God, and you knew everything and were in control of everything, you would be bored to death. It would be like making love to a plastic woman. Everything would be completely predictable, completely known, completely clear, no mystery, no surprise whatever.

Look at it another way. The object of our technology is to control the world, to have a superelectronic pushbutton universe, where we can get anything we want, fulfill any desires simply by pushing a button. You're Aladdin with the lamp, you rub it, the jinni comes and says, "Salaam, I'm your humble servant, what do you wish? Anything you want."

And after a while, just as in those dreams I described you would decide one day to forget that you were dreaming, you would say to the jinni of the lamp, "I would like a surprise." Or God, in the Court of Heaven, might turn to his vizier, and say, "Oh, Commander of the Faithful, we are bored." And the vizier of the Court would reply, "Oh King, live forever, surely out of the infinitude of your wisdom you can discover some way of not being bored." And the King would reply, "Oh vizier, give us a surprise." That's the whole basis of the story of the Arabian Nights. Here was a very powerful sultan, who was bored. And therefore he challenged Scheherazade to tell him a new story every night so that the telling of the tales, getting involved in adventures, would never, never end.

Isn't that the reason why we go to the theater, why we go to the movies, because we want to get out of ourselves? We want a surprise; and a surprise means that you have to *other* yourself. That is to say, there has to enter into your experience some element that is not under your control.

So if our technology were to succeed completely, and everything were to be under our control, we should eventually say, "We need a new button." With all these control buttons, we always have to have a button labeled SURPRISE, and just so it doesn't become too dangerous, we'll put a time limit on it—surprise for 15 minutes, for an hour, for a day, for a month, a year, a lifetime. Then, in the end, when the surprise circuit is finished, we'll be back in control and we'll all know where we are. And we'll heave a sigh of relief, but, after a while, we'll press the button labeled SURPRISE once more.

You will notice a curious rhythm to what I have been explaining, and this rhythm corresponds to the Hindu idea of the course of time and the way evolution works, an idea drastically different from ours. First of all, Hindus think of time as circular, as going round— look at your watch, it goes round. But Westerners tend to think of time in a straight line, a one-way street, and we got that idea from Hebrew religion, and from St. Augustine.

There is a time of creation, then a course of history which leads up to final, eschatological catastrophe, the end of the world, and after that, the judgment, in which all things will be put to right, all questions answered, and justice dealt out to everyone according to his merits. And that'll be that! Thereafter the universe will be, in a way, static; there will be the eternally saved and the eternally damned.

Now, many people may not believe that today, but that has been a dominating belief throughout the course of Western history, and it has had a tremendously powerful influence on our culture. But the Hindus think half of the world is going round and round for always, in a rhythm. They calculate the rounds in periods that in Sanskrit are called *kalpas,* and each kalpa lasts for 4,320,000 years. And so a kalpa is the period or *manvantara* during which the world as we know it is manifested. And it is followed by a period, also a kalpa long, 4,320,000 years, which is called *pralaya,* and this means when the world is not manifested anymore.

And these are the days and nights of Brahma, the godhead. During the manvantara when the world is manifested, Brahma is asleep, dreaming that he is all of us and everything that's going on, and during the pralaya, which is his day, he's awake, and knows himself, or itself (because it's beyond sex), for who and what he/she/it is. And then, once again, presses the button—surprise! As in the course of our dreaming, we would very naturally dream the most pleasant and rapturous dreams first and then get more adventurous, and experience and explore the more venturesome dimensions of experience.

In the same way, the Hindus think of a kalpa of the manifested universe, manvantara, as divided into four periods. These four periods are of different lengths. The first is the longest, and the last is the shortest. They are named in accordance with the throws in the Hindu game of dice. There are four throws and the throw of four is always the best throw, like the six in our game, the throw of one, the worst throw.

186

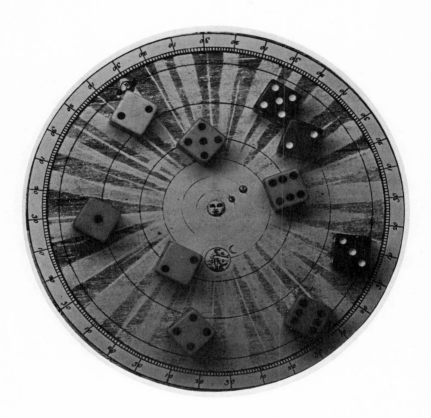

Now, therefore, the first throw is called *krita* and the epoch, the long, long period for which this throw lasts, is called a *yuga*. So we will translate yuga an epoch, and we will translate kalpa as an eon. Now the word *krita* means *done*, as when we say, "well done," and that is a period of the world's existence that we call the Golden Age when everything is perfect, done to perfection. When it comes to an end, we get *treta*-yuga that means *the throw of three*, and in this period of manifestation there's an element of the uncertain, an element of insecurity, an element of adventure in things. It's like a three-legged stool is not as secure as a four-legged one—you're a little more liable to be thrown off balance.

That lasts for a very long time, too, but then we get next what is called *dvapara*-yuga. *Dyam* means *two*, and in this period, the good and the bad, the pleasurable and the painful, are equally balanced. But, finally, there comes *kali*-yuga. Kali means *the worst throw*, and this lasts for the shortest time. This is the period of manifestation in which the unpleasurable, painful, diabolical principle finally takes over—but it has the shortest innings.

And at the end of the kali-yuga, the great destroyer of the worlds, God manifested as the destructive principle Shiva, does a dance called the *tandava*, and he appears, blue-bodied with ten arms, with lightning and fire appearing from every pore in his skin, and does a dance in which the universe is finally destroyed. The moment of cosmic death is the waking up of Brahma, the creator, for as Shiva turns round and walks off the stage, seen from behind, he is Brahma, the creator, the beginning of it all again. And Vishnu is the preserver, that is to say, the going on of it all, the whole state of the godhead being manifested as many, many faces. So, you see, this is a philosophy of the role of evil in life which is rational and merciful.

If we think God is playing with the world, has created it for his pleasure, and has created all these other beings and they go through the most horrible torments—terminal cancer, children being burned with napalm, concentration camps, the Inquisition, the horrors that human beings go through—how is that possibly justifiable? We try by saying, "Well, some God must have created it; if a God didn't create it, there's nobody in charge and there's no rationality to the whole thing. It's just a tale told by an idiot, full of sound and fury signifying nothing. It's a ridiculous system and the only out is suicide."

But suppose it's the kind of thing I've described to you, supposing it isn't that God is pleasing himself with all these victims, showing off his justice by either rewarding them or punishing them, supposing it's quite different from that. Suppose that God is the one playing all the parts, that God is the child being burned to death with napalm. There is no victim except the victor. All the different roles which are being experienced, all the different feelings which are being felt, are being felt by the one who originally desires, decides, wills to go into that very situation.

Curiously enough, there is something parallel to this in Christianity. There's a passage in St. Paul's Epistle to the Philippians in which he says a very curious thing: "Let this mind be in you which was also in Christ Jesus, who being in the form of God, did not think identity with God a thing to be clung to, but humbled himself and made himself of no reputation, and was found in fashion as a man and became obedient to death, even the death of the cross." Here you have exactly the same idea, the idea of God becoming human, suffering all that human beings can suffer, even death. And St. Paul is saying, "Let this mind be in you," that is to say, let the same kind of consciousness be in you that was in Jesus Christ. Jesus Christ knew he was God.

Wake up and find out eventually who you really are. In our culture, of course, they'll say you're crazy or you're blasphemous, and they'll either put you in jail or in the nut house (which is the same thing). But if you wake up in India and tell your friends and relations, "My goodness, I've just discovered that I'm God," they'll laugh and say, "Oh, congratulations, at last you found out."

PHILOSOPHICAL
FANTASIES

I am going to relate three fantasies, all of which have some- thing in common that will be evident to you at the end. The first fantasy is about reproduction. We use the word reproduction in two principal ways: We talk about the biological reproduction of a species, and we also speak of reproduction in terms of a painting, a photograph, a recording, a movie, or a videotape. Now what is reproduction in the latter all about? Well, hundreds of years ago, kings of Europe formed feudal alliances by marrying the princesses of far-off states. Before entering into a marriage contract they would have painters send portraits of the lady in question to see if his majesty approved of her. On one such occasion Henry the Eighth of England was badly cheated in this procedure by a too flattering portrait of Anne of Cleves.

Therefore, there developed a kind of moral code among artists in the European tradition beginning with the marvelous work of the Renaissance, and later the Flemish painters. Finally, with the Art Officiale of the 19th Century, we got what we now call photographic realism.

At that time they said, "Isn't there some more scientific way of doing this?" And so they discovered the camera. First there were those brownish daguerrotypes. People said, "Well, that is pretty, it really looks like grandpa, doesn't it?" "But," they said, "something, several things are missing; it isn't colored for one thing." So they tinted them.

And then they said, "Why, it's real lifelike, but you know, there are some people whose whole style of life, whose whole personality is in the way they move, and if you just take a static shot like that the personality isn't there." So they invented a way of making the images move—movies. I remember when the first movies came out they were all moving in a jerky way. They smoothed it out and everyone said, "Now that's real lifelike."

But after awhile they said, "But there's another thing missing which is sound; a whole lot of the personality is in the voice, so can't we have them talking at the same time that they move?" And someone invented the talkies; eventually they added color to them, and everyone said, "Wow, now we're really getting somewhere!" Then to make it even more real they put them in a three-dimensional process which required that you wear special spectacles to see.

But then people said, "Why is it that every time we want to see one of these things we have to go down to the center of town? Can't we have it all at home?" And so television was introduced; they started out with black and white and looking as Robert Benchley once described the cuts in French newspapers, as all looking as if they had been made on bread.

They improved it, colored it, and that's where we are now. Not quite. Because somebody has developed a thing that we shall all be seeing soon—the hologram—a television image produced by laser beams in which you see a three-dimensional figure out in the air in front of you. Soon we'll all say, "Now, isn't that marvelous!" But, of course, when you go up to it and put your hand on it, your hand goes right through it. You can't touch it. And, you see, that is the trouble with television—you look at whatever you're seeing behind a screen; but it's intangible, it doesn't smell, and it won't relate to you.

So there are future problems to be solved in the techniques of electronic reproduction—and they'll do it. They'll manage a way in which the electronic emission source can solidify and make the air vibrate so that you can touch the figure. You won't be able to push your hand through it because the air will be going faster than your hand. Imagine that! If there's a beautiful dancer on television, you'll actually be able to go up and embrace her. But she won't know you're there, she won't respond to you. And you'll say, "Well, that's not very lifelike," just as people once said,"If the photograph doesn't move it's not very lifelike, if it doesn't talk it's not very lifelike." They'll next say if the tangible, three-dimensional reproduction doesn't respond, it's not very lifelike, so they'll have to figure out a technique for doing that.

Will our technology be able to develop such a technique? Of course they will! Sitting in your home you will watch the scene on a kind of stage, not a screen, and there will be a TV camera observing you. That TV camera will report back everything you do into a computer and the computer will manage each bit of information going into the image that you're looking at, and will immediately decide what is the appropriate response to your approach to the image—and won't that be great! She may slap you in the face, or she may kiss you. You never know.

But eventually you'll say, "This is still not really the kind of reproduction I wanted. What I want is to be able to identify with one of the characters in the scene." We want not only to *watch* the drama that is being performed on the stage but actually to *get into* it. We will want to be wired in with electrodes on our brains that will actually allow us to feel the emotions of the people acting on the stage. Eventually we will get absolutely perfect reproductions and be able to see that image so vividly that we shall become it.

And so the question arises—could that be where we are already? Are we a reproduction which over the centuries of evolution has worked out to be a replica of something else that was going on and we are where we always were?

The second fantasy presents the idea that every living being thinks it's human, and that means a plant, a worm, a virus, a bacterium, a fruit fly, a hippopotamus, a giraffe, a rabbit. All beings whatever they feel out from, as we feel out from our bodies, feel that they're in the center. That is to say, wherever you look, you turn your head around and you feel you're the center of the world, you feel you're the center of the universe. Also, a rabbit or a fruit fly feels that it is the center. And it has around it a company of associates who look like it and therefore this creature knows that these are the right people, just as we know when we look at human beings they're the right people, they are one of us. Only, of course, we have to make distinctions because you never really know that you are you and are really in the right place unless you can compare and contrast yourself with some other people who are after all not quite in the right place and some other people who are very much in the wrong place. Through having this succession of comparisons, you know that you're OK.

Other animals and insects have exactly the same understanding of this arrangement. "Well," you say, "insects and things like fishes, they don't have any culture; what do you mean fishes are entitled to consider themselves in the same way as humans?" Let me present the argument from the fishes' point of view. Fishes think, "Human beings are a mess; look at what they do; they can't exist without cluttering themselves and carrying around all kinds of things outside their bodies; they have to have houses and automobiles and books and records and television and hi-fi equipment and stuff, endless stuff, and they litter the earth with rubbish.

Consider a dolphin's point of view (he isn't really a fish but a mammal) of the human race. Dolphins spend most of their time playing; they don't work because the grocery is right there in the ocean, whatever they need. A dolphin will catch up with a ship and get on the wake, putting its tail at an exact angle of 26°, and be carried along. The dolphin will make circles around the ship just for fun, playing all its life in the water. We know that a dolphin's brain is as big if not bigger than ours, that it is incredibly intelligent, and that it has a language which we can't decipher. The person who knows most about dolphins, Dr. John Lilly, is a friend of mine and he said he came to the conclusion that dolphins were too smart to tell us their language. So he abandoned this project. He said he would no longer keep such a highly civilized being in the concentration camp of a zoo, and that it should go back to the ocean. The point is, that every being, not only dolphins, but every organism that has any sensitivity in it whatsoever, considers itself to be the center of the universe.

Now this idea has its problems. There is a Zen poem which says, "The morning glory which blooms for an hour differs not at heart from a giant pine that lives for a thousand years." In other words, an hour is a long life to a morning glory, and a thousand years is a long life to a pine. And our four score and ten years or, as the insurance companies' actuarial tables put it, somewhere between 65 and 70 years as an average human life, seems about the right length of life. There are people who want to go on and on, who are impressed with immortality and have their bodies frozen in case there should develop in the future some technique by which they could be revived.

But I really don't agree with that idea because nature has mercifully arranged the principle of *forgettery* as well as the principle of memory. If you always and always remembered everything, you would be like a piece of paper which has been painted over and over until there was no space left and you wouldn't be able to distinguish between one thing and another. Or like a bunch of people screaming and making more and more noise until you can hear nobody. And in the same way one's memories become screams. Nature mercifully arranges for the whole thing to be erased so you can begin again.

It doesn't matter in what form you begin, whether you begin again as a human being, or as a fruit fly, or a beetle, or a bird, for it feels the same way that you feel now. So we're really all in the same place, we all have above us things much higher than ourselves, and we all have below us things that we feel are much lower than we. There are things out there on the left and things out there on the right, and things in front and things behind. You're the middle, you're the middle everywhere, always.

My third fantasy. It seems to me that nobody has really seriously asked the questions, "How do the stars begin?" "Why?" "How out of space do these enormous radioactive centers arise?" I'm going to solve this problem by using the analogy of the egg and chicken and say, "The chicken is one egg's way of becoming other eggs." And if you understand my second fantasy you know how that could be true. Now, let's suppose that a planet is one star's way of becoming another star. Stars, when they explode, send a lot of goo out into space and some of this goo solidifies into balls which get into orbit and spin round the star. And in one chance in a thousand, maybe, one of those balls will evolve like the planet Earth and slowly upon it will arise what some people might call a disease, the bacteria of intelligent life. And with them comes a notion, these things that we call alive, that they ought to go on. They have fixed ideas in their heads that they should keep on doing whatever it is they're doing and they should always be doing it better. They divide themselves into different species and these species compete with each other in order to, as it were, flex their muscles and get better and better at whatever it is they are. And they go on doing this until one species really establishes itself as top species on the particular planet just as we human beings, Homo sapiens, have established ourselves as top species on Earth, whatever top means.

Then, when we have a little leisure and don't have to spend all our time finding food to put into our mouths, we start asking questions. We look around at each other and everything and say, "What is this? What is going on here?" Some people say, "That's a stupid question to ask. Why don't you just go on doing your work. Go hunting, go farming, go doing your business." But we persist, "No, there are higher things." And thereby create a special class of people who in India are called Brahmans, among us philosophers, scientists, theologians, thinkers. And because they go into the question of why we are here they are allowed to stop farming, to stop hunting, to stop mining, to stop scrubbing floors, and they go to very special places called universities where they can sit around and think about what is going on. They do what is called philosophy, which means they try to say what it means. What does the word *be* mean, what does the word *exist* mean? What do we mean when we say *we're here*? They find they can't discuss that very far because the word stops meaning anything, it sort of becomes a noise.

They say, "Now, we're not really getting to the point, what we've got to do is instead of thinking all the time, theorizing and talking words about what's going on, we've got to investigate it experimentally. We've somehow got to look into this stuff that we call reality, the material world, and find out what it is. So they start chopping it up. They dissect flowers, they chop up the seeds and look into the middle of them. They find something there and then they have to get a magnifying glass to examine that and break it down into smaller and smaller pieces and reason they must eventually come to some particle called an atom. In Greek, *atomos*, or atom, means noncuttable, what you can't split any further. So they come down to the atomos, that than which there is no whicher—they thought! But then they found they could split the atom, they could find the electron, the positron, the meson, etc., etc., etc., forever.

Eventually they determined that every atomos of matter contains immense energy and that such energy could be released. The trouble with intellectual people is that anything that can be done must be done. And in the necessary course of the development of nature they found out how to blow the Earth to pieces and turn it into a star.

So that may be how stars originate. They have planets like chickens have eggs, and the eggs burst and turn into chickens. And planets burst through the agency of intelligent life and turn into stars which throw out other mudballs, some of which stand a reasonable chance of giving rise to new intelligent life, about as reasonable a chance as any male spermatozoan stands when it enters the female womb of becoming a baby—one in a million.

Now you may think this is a rather unpleasant fantasy. You may feel that things are going the wrong way, the wrong direction. If the whole point of life, this tender biological substance with all its tubes and filaments and nerves which are so very sensitive, if all this is to end up in fire, into an absolute blaze of light, won't that be a shame? Is that the way it all ends?

Many people say they want to see the light, they want to be enlightened, they want to dissolve into the light of God. Then when they've succeeded in doing just that (all over again) the process goes on, and the exploding Earth/star blows out those mudballs, and planets are created and once again you're a baby, you're a child, the flowers are brilliantly colored, the stars are gorgeous, the smell of the earth, the sound of the rain, everything is marvelous once again. And once again you see the other, the man, the woman that you love as if it had never happened before, it all starts over again.

And as it goes on it gets more and more intense, the problems
get more and more problematic, you find you are wrestling
with something you can't control. You've got to control it,
but you absolutely can't control it. Like all the problems of
the world at the present time, the whole scene is completely
out of hand. We feel we are going to our doom because once
again we are going towards the birth of a star which is the
most creative thing there is.

Now think about these for awhile, these three fantasies which
all have a cyclic quality. And to them I want to add a note
about biological reproduction. When I think back to my
grandfather whom I knew fairly well, when I was a little boy,
he was something extraordinarily impressive. He looked like
King Edward VII. He was a very, very elegant man with a
little goatee beard. He didn't have sideburns as I do, and he
had shorter hair—a very elegant fellow, dressed beautifully.
And I thought he was the very image of God. Here I am the
same age as he was when I first knew him, and I have five
grandchildren, and I am sort of no longer impressed by
grandfathers! I'm one of them too! And this is the same idea
of the cycle that we are almost perpetually in the same place
as the French proverb says, *Plus ca change, plus c'est la
meme chose*—The more it changes, the more it's the same.

That means then that existence, the feeling of being, is a sort of spectrum just as light is a spectrum, at one end red and at the other end violet, and you have these extremes in order to have color at all, in order to know light. So you see, likewise we have to have the experience that there is somebody else, something else going on altogether out of our control in order to have the experience of being me. And so in order to feel good, to feel that life is worthwhile, that existence is worth going on with, in order to bring out that feeling just as the red brings out the violet, there has to be in the back of our minds, maybe very far away, the comprehension that there is something that could happen, that absolutely must not happen, that is the horrors, that is the *screaming-meemies-at-the-end-of-the-line*.

We have to know that's there, like just before he died the British novelist Arnold Bennett said, "I feel somehow that everything is absolutely wrong." And so the possibility, even the imagination, that there could be such an experience in the back of our heads is the background which gives intensity to the sense that we call feeling good, feeling that it's all right.

So if you understand that you are, really and truly, always in the same place, just as every creature thinks it's a human being and just as every being turns out to be a reproduction by some interesting technology, whether it's electronic or biological makes very little difference, then you understand the nature of life. And just as planets may be stars' ways of becoming other stars, you're always in the same place. And what is that place? You can ask yourself very, very—I won't say seriously because it really isn't serious, it's sincere—ask yourself very sincerely, if that is so, if the place in which you are now is the place where everything and everybody else really is.

Only there's an arrangement to pretend that you ought to be somewhere else, so the place where you are is the place where you are always pretending you ought to be somewhere else. This is the nature of life, this is the pulse. *I ought to be somewhere else.* If you discover that that's the trick you're playing on yourself, you become serene and you don't entirely give up the game because you've seen through it. You say, "Hmm, it really might be fun to go on playing."

These talks by Alan Watts are also available on audio cassettes from:

The Electronic University
Box 361
Mill Valley, CA 94941

For a catalog of the audio library of Alan Watts' lectures and seminars write to:

MEA
Box 303
Sausalito, CA 94965

OTHER BOOKS by ALAN WATTS

The Spirit of Zen
The Meaning of Happiness
The Theologia Mystica of St. Dionysius
Behold the Spirit
The Supreme Identity
The Wisdom of Insecurity
Myth and Ritual in Christianity
The Way of Liberation in Zen Buddhism
The Way of Zen
Nature, Man, and Woman
This Is It
Psychotherapy East and West
The Joyous Cosmology
The Two Hands of God
Beyond Theology: The Art of Godmanship
Nonsense
The Book: On the Taboo Against Knowing
Who You Are
Does It Matter? Essays on Man's Relation to Materiality
Erotic Spirituality
In My Own Way: An Autobiography
The Art of Contemplation